How NOT to Lead

How NOT to Lead

Lessons Every Manager Can Learn from Dumpster Chickens, Mushroom Farmers, and Other Office Offenders

Chase Cunningham

WILEY

This book is dedicated to those who will come into the cybersecurity and technology industry as leaders. You are the future, and you owe it to yourself and your future employees to be the best leader you can be.

This book is also dedicated to the Dumpster Chickens, Mushroom Farmers, and bad leaders I've had the benefit of working with and for in the past. Your attitude, aptitude, and general jackassery inspired me to help others and not to be you.

Contents

Contents

Introduction

I've learned something too: selling out is sweet because, when you sell it out, you get to make a lot of money; you don't have to hang out with a bunch of poor losers like you guys.
—Eric Cartman, *South Park*

Okay, let me start by saying I am not a sellout. At least I don't think I am. I hope I'm not, anyway. I don't do "on poz" keyboard red team guy work anymore, so I guess maybe I have achieved peak poser status, but I am no sellout. I still love the in-the-trenches work for cyber. Anyway, I love that quote from Cartman about selling out and making money. I think that's what you get from most leadership and self-help books; there are hundreds of armchair experts waving their hands, talking about gaining insight from walking on hot coals and playing on people's emotions rather than their logic. I've read many of those books and watched their YouTube videos for research, and I assert that most of them are preying on people's fear of failure and desire to do something that matters. It's the same crap as "fitness" industry influencers claiming that miracle supplements of ground-up tree bark and wombat spit will make us as ripped as they are if we pay them for the privilege of ingesting junk.

The truth is, it's been decades since most swamis and gurus did the actual work they preach to you about. They made their one shot, cashed in, and can testify to their "vast" knowledge of the current problem. Even though they stopped doing the work, they lecture us about what they did back then. Sure, they might have some insight, and we could benefit from some of their thinking, but let's be honest. They aren't in the trenches doing the work today. And that's where the real value comes from.

That's why I wanted to write *How NOT to Lead*. I am in the trenches—maybe not writing code or banging away at networks anymore, but I am still there in the muck, working with companies to grow and win in the space. As I am writing this, I am like many of you. I am trying to raise a family, build a company (more than one), contribute to the community, and learn from my mistakes. I am truly blessed to have those opportunities, but I am also blessed because I have been uniquely positioned to learn from some of the worst leaders in the military and business worlds. Yeah, you read that right. Blessed because of the worst leaders.

I am also blessed to have seen some of the best leaders out there do the job in the military or the corporate world. As an analyst at a major analyst firm, I worked with hundreds of companies; and as a contractor, I have run across even more as I traverse the technology space. I am on the board of more than a dozen companies, and I will chat with between 6 and 10 different companies this week about their corporate technology strategies.

To be blunt, I have seen it all. At least, I have certainly seen enough to know what not to do.

Most of us either wound up in a leadership position or took over because no one else would. Regardless of how we got there, we are there now, and part of being a leader is getting better at it. That's where these stories come in.

In this book, I will tell you about people who have faced challenges, made difficult decisions, and experienced both victories and setbacks. Those on-the-ground insights are based on actual scenarios, making that advice relatable and actionable.

I will detail practical perspectives and thinking that self-help gurus might not possess (no matter what they say in their marketing). I will not bullshit you with flowery talk or preach at you.

One of the most powerful aspects of learning is gaining insights from failures—and trust me, I have failed and seen failure. In the real world, not every decision leads to success, and leaders who openly discuss their failures provide valuable lessons in resilience, adaptability, and learning from mistakes.

Effective leadership is highly contextual. What works in one industry, company, or situation might not be applicable elsewhere, but there are basic tenets that we can and should align ourselves with. By analyzing some major leadership snafus and oopsies, I will help you better understand how different thinking and diverse contexts can help you adapt your leadership principles.

I am not a social sciences expert. I am not a self-help guru or a professional leadership coach. I am a retired Navy Chief, a technologist, a security wonk, a student of experience, and a keen observer of success and failure. I want to help provide you with insights into what you shouldn't do to succeed as a technology market leader.

Leadership is a journey filled with challenges, uncertainties, and unexpected turns. As a leader in this dynamic space, the path to success isn't solely illuminated by shining examples of triumphant ventures. It's often the cautionary tales, the missteps, and the downright bizarre encounters that shape our understanding of effective leadership.

In this uniquely titled guide, I break away from the conventional wisdom of leadership to embrace the unconventional—from dumpster chickens who dive in and crap all over their people, to mushroom farmers who keep their people in the dark and shovel manure on their efforts; nothing is off the table. While the tech world surges forward with innovation and ambition, the leadership journey is scattered with pitfalls and peculiarities that defy convention. By reading this book, you will learn the truth behind those issues and failures and gain insight into how to avoid those calamities.

Each chapter of this book introduces you to a concept or character related to the tech industry and educates you about what they did to avoid failure or help you understand where they ignored the warnings and essentially chose failure. As we venture into the world of these office offenders, we'll explore their escapades, analyze their mistakes and extract the wisdom they unknowingly offer to those willing to listen.

As you flip through the pages of *Lessons Every Manager Can Learn from Dumpster Chickens, Mushroom Farmers, and Other Office Offenders*, you'll encounter not only obvious pitfalls—the tech startups that soared too close to the sun or the giants that faltered in their adaptability—but also quirky and unexpected stories that hold hidden gems of insight. We'll delve into the lives of unconventional teachers and differing concepts we should embrace to be better leaders and managers.

The world of leadership isn't neat and polished; it's a muddy, dirty tapestry woven from a multitude of experiences, both mundane and extraordinary. By learning from unusual sources and being open to different ways of thinking, you'll be better equipped to navigate challenges, anticipate pitfalls, and emerge as a more effective and adaptable leader in the technology market.

So, brace yourself for a journey that will take you from the mundane to the surreal and maybe even the asinine. You will learn from the predictable to the unexpected and from the tech world's triumphs to its humorous and humbling misadventures (including some of my own).

Join me as we unearth the wisdom that emerges when we dare to learn from the most unlikely of mentors: the dumpster chickens, mushroom farmers, and other office offenders who offer unconventional yet invaluable lessons in leadership.

How NOT to Lead

CHAPTER

1

The Value of Knowing What NOT to Do

Experience is knowing what not to do and knowing when not to do it.

—Dennis Coates

Experience is the best teacher anyone will ever have. Pain is one of the best educators any person has ever met. Think about it for a second. Remember the first time you touched something hot? It probably only took once for you to learn, "If the pan is hot; I should not touch it." Odds are, if you're like me, you were a smart-ass kid who looked your parents directly in the face as they told you, "Don't touch that; it's hot." And what did you and I do? We reached out with smug smiles and grabbed that hot pan. And immediately, the lesson became exponentially evident: We should listen. In the half-second it took for the electric signal to travel from our fingertips up our arm, across our chest, up through our neck, and into our tiny childish brains, we were made aware of the truth that our parents weren't lying to us and that the pan was indeed hot. We were learning in real time that we should not do things that would cause us harm, and we were being educated to trust that those older and more experienced than us were warning us for a very good reason.

Unfortunately for me, I am hardheaded. Although I learned from the hot-pan problem the first time, it would take a potentially life-threatening event for me to learn that I should not ignore the cautions of those who know what they are doing and have the life experience to justify their cautions.

I'm from Texas. I grew up on a farm. Well, a ranch. The nearest town has a whopping population of fewer than 400 people, and I graduated high school with a massive class of 51 students other than myself. In our school, everyone played all the sports, and everyone had to be engaged in every after-school activity simply because there weren't enough people to fill a bus to attend any events. For the district to pay for the gas for us to have an educational program after school, everyone participated whether we liked it or not. It was a town with only three streets and no stoplights. The firefighters operated out of a barn, and in the fall, you were allowed to bring your shotgun to school to go dove hunting in the afternoons. It was as Texas as it comes.

I still love to go home and be with my family on the farm, and I honestly think that's one of the places where I learned some of my most valuable lessons about what not to do and when to listen to people who know what the hell is going on. When you live on a ranch, ultimately, you will have to work the cattle. What does this mean for all you city slickers? Well, it means eventually, you're going to take the herd, no matter how large it is, and get it into a corral and begin to give the cattle all the medications, vaccinations, and treatments they need to stay healthy. The money generated from the sale of those animals feeds your family, and you have no choice but to make sure they are as healthy as possible so they can get to market.

A rite of passage for most Texas boys is finally getting to work the herd with their father. And just like every other kid in my small town, I couldn't wait for the day I got to work the herd with dad. You had to be physically large enough to be helpful, so you couldn't work the cows until you got to be at least 10 or 11. Luckily, I was a big kid. The first time I did this, I was about 11 years old, and I was tall enough that dad was ready to have me help him work the herd. In Texas, you do this in the spring when the weather goes from cool in the morning to boiling hot in the afternoon. You get sunburned, the air smells like shit and burnt leather, and the experience is genuinely unpleasant. Working the herd is nothing like the romantic scenes you've seen in movies like *Lonesome Dove* or the TV show *Yellowstone*. But it's something that every Texas boy who has access to a ranch and animals wants to do.

The first time I went to the annual roundup, cowboy hat in hand, ready to help dad and other ranchers work on the cows and prepare the herd for the next year, I was excited. I was unafraid, and I was ready to show them that I was a young man and could help do these things, just like the rest of the cowboys. Like every other time before when I had watched from afar, things seemed normal. The herd was driven into the corral, the animals were lined up, and we got ready to begin with the yearlings (cows between one and two years old) at the front of the line for processing. Some cows get big fast and can easily be north of 350 pounds in their first year, but the yearlings are "manageable" as they are smaller.

While these animals look like big, slow, lumbering oafs, they are not. When you take a few thousand pounds of beef and throw it into a corral, and the herd gets the idea that something is going wrong—they can hear the moans and bellows of their fellow cows as they are being treated, injected, and stuck with a variety of sharp metal objects—their stress levels go through the roof. The yearlings are exceptionally prone to this stress and will do anything to find a way to get out of that corral as fast as possible. (Keep this in mind.) My job as the low man on the totem pole but also the largest kid in the corral was to help push the yearlings up through the corral into a narrow channel or chute that would ultimately bring them in front of the real cowboys who would treat each yearling as it emerged. Sounds simple enough, right?

On my first go-round, I got behind a group of a few yearlings, started whooping and hollering like all the other cowboys, and watched as the herd began to move up into the chute. All was well. "This work is alright; I could do this all day long," I thought to myself. And then the situation began to change. Fast. About the third yearling in line figured out that things were not going to go well for it when it got to the end of the chute. The yearling decided unexpectedly to do a complete 180 and come back out at full speed, directly toward me. If you've never been in a position where a mass of beef is running at you as fast as possible and you have nowhere to go, it's a terrifying experience. Being a young man and typically doing things like reacting rather than thinking, I did what any self-preserving human would do and jumped toward the nearest fence as 500 pounds of beef rocketed past me.

It was probably one of the fastest moves I have ever made in this life, but that quick move resulted in removing the only barrier between the rest of the yearlings and their freedom. In seconds, they discovered they could backtrack out of that chute, and they rushed me in a wave of hoofs and muscle that my young mind could barely comprehend. Before I could turn around to face the chute again, the yearlings knocked me over, trampled me, and kicked me in the face as they vaulted out of the chute. As I've said, I have a hard head, and nothing other than my pride got seriously hurt. But now I had to push the same animals back into this chute.

The problem was that while cows are simple, they aren't stupid, and now they were aware that they had the power and ability to backtrack out of that uncomfortable place at will. Effectively, the beef was now in charge of the situation and process. So, for the next 8 or 10 hours, one by one, I had to grab a yearling, physically shove it into the chute, and then hold it in position until the cowboys were ready to process it. Our herd at that time was a few hundred cows, which also meant there were a few hundred yearlings, so my friend Gary Lee and I spent the entirety of that day and the next two days getting our asses kicked, stomped on, and shat on simply because I had not stood my ground with the first yearlings I faced.

Where does knowing what not to do come into this conversation? Why am I telling you a story about some redneck kid doing rancher stuff in a book about leadership? Before this engagement, we had a cowboy named Sidney who had been doing cowboy things his entire life. He had the craggy hands, leather skin, and scraggly beard of a man who had spent a lifetime doing hard, physical work. Sidney could easily have been an extra on *Yellowstone*. In the days before we began to move the herd into the corral, Sidney tried to advise me never to back up, knowing that I would be the low man on the totem pole who would push the yearlings into the chute. With a cigarette hanging out of his mouth and a bullwhip in his hand, already three beers deep on the morning before that day in the corral, he looked me dead in the face and said, "Never back up, because if you do, they're going to know they can lick you. They'll figure it out quick, boy. And you're going to spend the rest of your time doing these one by one. And you will get your ass stomped."

I acknowledged Sidney's words smugly, but I did not heed them. I smiled at him and tipped my hat like any good cowboy would do, but his words passed through my ears like a Taco Bell burrito moving through a freshman's colon. Someone who had the experience and knew the issues I was about to face had told me what not to do: "Do not give those animals an inch. Do not back up. Above all, keep the yearlings with their heads facing forward, and keep pressure on them so they won't move anywhere but where we want them to go." Had I done those things, I would not have spent three days straight moving animals one by one into and out of the chute in the blazing Texas heat.

But what does that lesson have to do with business and knowing what not to do? The lesson I learned that day (aside from how corral dirt tastes) was that even though someone might not be the boss (Sidney was a hand, not the corral boss), those seasoned in the work know what they are talking about and should be listened to. The people who have done and are doing the work have the insight and knowledge that is only learned by failing at something repeatedly. I learned right there, with my face down in the dust and cow crap, that lessons from the people who have been in the trenches have immense value.

In my interactions and workshops with executives, I have seen that this insight is usually woefully absent. I have been in rooms with the highly paid, highly educated executive staff and watched them ignore the advice and lessons of those who weren't present or, worse, were in the room and were blatantly ignored because the muckety-mucks were "solving bigger problems." Okay, maybe they are. Maybe they are thinking on a different plane, but the odds are that they still should perk their ears up. The people who have the scars from doing the actual job know what works and what doesn't.

I am sure that this sounds like "duh" to you. You would think so, but I have found that all of us, especially those in senior leadership positions, spend most of our time with our heads in the clouds trying to solve the "big problems." I have been in rooms where the person who does the work and has the scars to prove it chimes in on an issue, and although the people in the room don't overtly discount their input (that would be rude), they don't give the person the credit they are due.

You may not get the big idea or the game-changer concept from the people who do the work and make things happen. But at all costs, don't ignore their input. They know what not to do. They have cut their teeth on that misery biscuit and can guide your organization's thinking about what pitfalls you are facing. It's a lesson I learned as a young man after getting my ass stomped for days on end, but I only had to learn it once. Take your time, and listen to those further down the corporate food chain. They may not be the boss, just as Sidney was not, but they can save you considerable pain.

So don't ignore the folks who do the work, especially the older or more seasoned people who know where the bodies are buried. But what about a different example of a senior leader realizing things at the corporate and macroeconomic levels? Are there any examples of a corporate legend observing that everything was wrong and failure was imminent and then making a dramatic change by realizing what not to do? Yup. But I doubt you would think that Steve Jobs is one of the greatest examples of exactly this approach.

If you read books on technology, sooner or later you'll see references to Steve Jobs. It's rare to read anything in technology about products, innovation, or changing the world and not encounter a mention of Steve Jobs. The man rightly deserves all the credit he's been given, as he did essentially change the world. Hell, I have multiple Apple products in my home right now. I use my Apple Watch at the gym. All my photos are stored in my iCloud, and my iPhone is the digital leash that I am constantly tethered to, but that technology also provides me immense value. Steve Jobs was an intelligent businessman and innovator whose focus on the customer and the product was not seen in the market before he did it. But he was an asshole. And not just a regular one; he was a jerk of epic proportions. His leadership style was such that when employees saw him coming down the hall at his own company, they would find a way to turn and go in a different direction so they did not run into him. Steve Jobs had a small, close-knit group of people who would willingly interact with him even though his wrath was always just a few breaths away. Later in this book, we'll talk about the issues around being a jerk and why that's another no-no for any business leader, but I felt it was appropriate to state for once that Steve Jobs was an asshole. Another life goal achieved.

What can we learn from Steve Jobs that can tell us what not to do? Jobs once said, "Deciding what not to do is as important as deciding what to do." Never were words like that more valid than when Steve Jobs came back to take over Apple Computer in 1997. When he was brought back to help revamp the company, Jobs quickly realized that there were over a dozen different product lines all simultaneously competing in the market. After less than a month of being back on the job, Jobs saw that the way Apple Computer was going about its current business meant it was facing calamity.

Steve Jobs was forced out of Apple Computer in 1985. When it happened, his departure was not much more than a blip on most business radars. He did what promising innovators and entrepreneurs do: left that company and went on with another venture. Although tales of his ousting are the stuff of legend and have a kind of Shakespearean narrative to them, when he was let go, Jobs was noted to have raged at the board with a fury that "scared the shit out of everyone," according to an executive who was present at that uncomfortable meeting.

Following his abrupt departure, Apple Computer's new leadership began to focus on creating technology by combining the

Macintosh computer, the LaserWriter desktop printer, and Aldus PageMaker (later part of Adobe Systems) into a stream of capabilities that would be offered to the market in the mid-1980s. These efforts were all put in motion with the additional objective of Apple Computer maintaining at least 55 percent of the overall market share. And for a while, Apple Computer ran the market. Its numbers and growth were aligned with expectations, and all was well in the Apple Computer kingdom. But that level of production and development combined with compounding capabilities inevitably leads to product sprawl and the increase in price that tracks along with it. IBM PC computers and compatibles introduced essentially the same functionality at an exceptionally lower price, which effectively gutted Apple Computer's position and dominance in the market.

While this combat was taking place between Apple Computer and IBM PC computers, Steve Jobs founded and ran NeXT, Inc. Jobs founded this company to focus on powerful technology that could run enterprise-level applications but was still affordable enough that a college student could purchase one of the machines and use it in their dorm room. While that was a great idea, the overall price of a NeXT computer was more than $10,000, and most college kids didn't have enough money for Taco Bell, much less $10,000 for a nifty box-size computer. NeXT sold only about 50,000 of these machines, most to large government organizations that could afford such a hefty price tag for a sexy, cool workstation. The real innovation NeXT was offering was the operating system, which would introduce the concept of object-oriented programming into the personal computing space. That object-oriented programming innovation ultimately led to the Mac OS X operating system, the game changer in the computer space, when Apple Computer acquired Steve Jobs' company and ported its operating system over.

Once Jobs came back into the Apple Computer family, it did not take long for him to change the company's approach. In less than a month of being back on campus, Jobs realized that there was too much going on for successful execution. Apple Computer was trying to compete at an unachievable price point with technology that was excessively complicated and overpriced for a market that only needed some of the things it sold. The story goes that in one of his many fits of rage, Jobs stood up during a product meeting and drew a square carved into quadrants on a whiteboard. At the top of the quadrant, He wrote "consumer and professional," and on the other axis of the quadrant, he wrote "desktop and portable." Then he turned to everyone in the room and said, "Anything not in those quadrants is canceled." With that simple statement, Steve Jobs effectively canceled 70 percent of Apple Computer's current product line. After a period of stunned silence, the people in the room filtered out, tiptoeing away from the space so as not to incur Jobs' wrath further, went back to their respective work centers, and delivered the news.

Not long after that, Steve Jobs realized that Apple Computer corporate was facing another problem that was undercutting the company's ability to execute and grow. He analyzed the corporate earnings and P&L statements and uncovered a concerning fact. Essentially, he realized that the way the company was accounting for P&L statements among the organizations within Apple Computer needed to be revised. Obliterated was more like it. Because of the fragmented and overly bureaucratic approach, every business unit at Apple Computer had its own individual P&L statement.

Originally, profit and loss were calculated within Apple Computer by each business unit. That accounting and performance strategy was a siloed and micro-focused approach, leading to infighting among the divisions as each tried to determine where to allocate its costs. Managers were only concerned with their units showing a profit, which meant they were in truth ignoring the company's overall health. They could not see the forest for the trees. Jobs realized this was a critical flaw and only hampered growth and cooperation; he decided, "We won't do this anymore." To fix this problem and remove the primary failure point, he upended the company's management structure. Jobs eliminated every manager at Apple Computer, blew up the complicated business operations, and moved the company away from a practice that made sense for the IRS but not for Apple Computer. His move away from that failure also aided Apple Computer in moving to a model of only one P&L statement for the company, which ultimately improved the company's position and optimized reporting for the accounting group.

Adopting that changed functional structure was innovative for a company like Apple Computer. But thanks to the "We aren't doing business this way anymore" focus of Steve Jobs, Apple still operates this way, even though it is now nearly 40 times as large in revenue and quintupled in headcount. Senior vice presidents oversee the specific functions of the teams, not the output of the products. Steve Jobs died in 2011, but the new CEO, Tim Cook, still occupies the only position on the organizational chart where the design, engineering, operations, marketing, and sales of any of Apple's main products converge. Other than the CEO, the company operates without conventional general managers. No people control the entire process, from product development through sales, and no work centers are judged according to a P&L statement.

So, what's the takeaway from this story? Why do we need another rundown of something unique that Steve Jobs did? You might be thinking, "I thought this was going to be a book about how not to do things." Exactly. By knowing what not to do, such as keeping 40 different product lines all running at the same time, none of which were delivered to customers in a manner that benefited them, Steve Jobs realized that he needed to draw a line in the sand to say "We're not doing this anymore." By coming back into the company and helping the leadership understand that what they were doing was drowning the company, Steve Jobs ultimately optimized the corporate approach. He changed the accounting practices for one of the most profitable companies on the planet.

Had he not done so, Apple Computer would have continued along its path and ultimately missed becoming a dominant force in computing. The desktop computer space would have passed it. Had he not realized that there were things the company should not be engaging in and that there were only a few exceptionally viable routes to the market, nothing would have changed. There would be no iPhone. There would be no Apple Watch. There would be no iCloud. If ever there was a great example of someone in a leadership position stepping up and realizing what not to do, this is it.

A great example in the cybersecurity market of knowing what not to do and ignoring those warnings comes from observations around the company formerly known as Norse Corp. Norse Corp is one of the most significant examples of how everything that could have gone right for a company went wrong as soon as Norse Corp's kimono was rolled open. How did a company that had the money, marketing, and technology (or so it seemed) not heed the warnings in the fishbowl market of cybersecurity that all of us have heard repeatedly: "Never lie about your technology in a space filled with hackers whose sole purpose in life has been to find flaws and weaknesses in systems"?

In 2012, Norse Corp was known as a cybersecurity industry darling, racking up massive investment, exponential growth, and new clients at an almost unachievable pace. Norse Corp was doing so well that it had the money to hire actors in Viking costumes to show up at various cybersecurity conferences. The real sexy factor for Norse Corp's technology was its attack map graph, which was quickly adopted by various organizations as their view into the cyber underground. This map was produced in real time and could show a variety of attacks globally targeting infrastructure. It was a well-crafted, sexy map that drew the eye of anyone who happened to come across it. However, that was about as deep as the technology went for Norse Corp.

For four years, Norse Corp was trucking along, doing what all startups want to do: gaining customers and growing. Norse Corp accumulated tens of millions of dollars of funding, which at the time was an excessive amount of investment for a small startup in cybersecurity. Norse Corp was also one of the most active threat-intelligence reporting groups and was deeply engaged with various media outlets. When Sony was hacked in 2014, Norse Corp was the first organization to be on the news talking about the link to a malicious insider. A source of information known only to Norse Corp corroborated the reporting. Norse Corp also published research specifically citing cyberattacks against critical infrastructure that Norse Corp had attributed to Iran. Again, the company's analysis and data were the only sources for that unique insight. Somewhere, alarm bells began to ring, even as Norse Corp grew in the market and continued producing various intelligence reports. But much like Icarus, Norse Corp was getting too close to the sun.

In 2014, Norse Corp was throwing amazing parties at a variety of top Internet security conferences and luring dozens of security experts to come work for the company. One was Mary Landesman, a former senior security researcher at Cisco Systems. Landesman was brought to Norse Corp to be its chief data scientist, and she was so certain about the company's success that she even recruited her son to work at Norse Corp. As the lead data scientist, Landesmann's job was to discover valuable and interesting patterns in the "real-time attack data and cyber threat intelligence telemetry" that Norse Corp was famous for. However, it wasn't until seven months after she was hired as Norse Corp's chief data scientist that Landesman was provided access to the data that it was part of her job to analyze. To put it bluntly, she was disappointed in the quality and integrity of the data she finally received. She noted that the information she was provided was little more than anyone might glean from an exposed, public-facing web server that was misconfigured. She was quoted as saying, "The data isn't great, and it's pretty much the same thing as if you looked for web server logs that had automated crawlers and scanning tools hitting it constantly." Adding to this failure, Landesman noted that the way Norse Corp collected its data was a protected secret, and only the top three people in the company were provided access to those data streams.

When Norse Corp published its analysis of the industrial control system attacks and attributed those attacks to Iran, the analysis was called into suspicion. Rob Lee, considered one of the greatest minds in the space around industrial cybersecurity controls, gutted the entirety of the Norse Corp analysis on the Iranian critical infrastructure hacks, calling it disingenuous at best and potentially inflammatory at worst. In Rob's counteranalysis, he was quoted as saying, "The systems in question are fake, and the data obtained cannot be accurately used for attribution. In essence, Norse identified scans from Iranian Internet locations against fake systems and announced them as attacks launched by the Iranian government."

In 2016, Norse Corp's CEO was asked to step down by the board of directors. In a rather abrupt series of events, the company went from live and thriving to offline over three days. It turned out that the majority of Norse Corp analysis was bullshit. Its unique insights and detailed analysis of data streams that only Norse Corp could acquire were nothing more than recalibrated, slightly modified narratives that Norse Corp employees crafted to meet the growing demand from investors and the media. In various critical analyses from deeply educated technical experts in the cybersecurity space, Norse Corp's assertions were eviscerated. Rob Lee is also the co-founder of security software maker Dragos Security, now a billion-dollar cyber unicorn, and a former cyberwarfare operations officer for the U.S. Air Force. He posted a blog stating that Norse Corp was "not a bellwether of the threat intel industry. While their product and Internet level scanning data was interesting and potentially very valuable for research it was not threat intelligence. So while they may have billed themselves as significant players in the threat intelligence community, they were never really accepted by the community, or participating in it, by most leading analysts and companies."

Brian Krebs, a well-known reporter in cybersecurity, also took Norse Corp to task, revealing that its insights into a malicious insider at Sony were nothing more than rumors and gossip. Weeks after Norse Corp asserted to the media that its analysis of the Sony hack indicated a malicious insider, the FBI released federal indictments against various North Korean hackers, proving Norse Corp's assertions were incorrect. Additionally, Norse Corp's threat intelligence map was found to be little more than basic Internet searches that had been repackaged to look like an attack map. Norse Corp's map was jokingly called the "Pew Pew" map within the cyber community space.

At the time of all its hype, Norse Corp stated that the data it used to feed its online attack map came from a combination of over 8 million sensors and honeypot systems that the company had meticulously put in place in more than 47 international locations to gather and collate a variety of enemy attack data. However, as soon as the company began to implode, essentially because there was too much money going out the door and not enough coming in, some departing employees noted that while

Norse Corp data was potentially valuable, the leadership of the company was not interested in investing in operationalizing that data. Those departing employees stated that the leadership was satisfied with the interactivity and visuals of the "Pew Pew" map. Following the company's collapse, the map's developers publicly stated that there were serious questions about the validity of the data behind the map itself.

Norse Corp went from being a cybersecurity company with the sky as its limit to gone overnight. But outside of the suspicious fundraising and founder shenanigans (which seems to happen with many companies in cyber), what factors sealed their fate? What sin did the company commit in the eyes of the industry that it should have known not to commit? Norse Corp simply did not heed the warnings from the most significant leaders and contributors in the small community that is cybersecurity.

For years, Norse Corp made it a point to go for broke against the advice of its own board members, several of whom came with deep experience in the cyber community. Despite constant gentle notifications from its own personnel and its partners that Norse Corp was not being well received by the broader cybersecurity community, Norse Corp blatantly disregarded the warnings and indications. It was about to be "outed" by an industry built by people who pride themselves on discovering weaknesses and vulnerabilities in both systems and businesses. Norse Corp could have cloaked its shady business dealings and fundraising behind the veil of VC financing, as many other companies have, and continued without much interruption, but it should have known not to pee in the small swimming pool that is cybersecurity. Amid all the questions, accusations, and constant barrage of conversations around the company's technology and the validity of its most prized offering, the attack map, the leadership at Norse Corp should have taken the time to step back and ask themselves, "Should we keep doing this the way we are?"

As with the parable of my own painful lesson about listening to the more experienced folks who are in the trenches doing the work, Norse Corp leaders never took a pause and read the room. Had they done that, they would have noticed the following:

- Employees were openly criticizing and questioning the company's product value.
- Most cybersecurity insiders were also poking at the weaknesses in the company's offering and public presence.
- The company received a frigid reception at industry events and conferences.
- The CEO and CTO had to publicly defend the value proposition of the "Pew Pew" map at every turn.
- At industry events, the company hired actors in full Viking regalia who were met with outright laughter.

Sure, if you look at the entirety of the cybersecurity space, you can find companies that have goofy marketing campaigns, and you can certainly find companies that aren't well received by the community. But Norse Corp set the standard, and at every turn, it chose to ignore the inputs it was receiving. If what your company is doing makes your employees feel as if the community they are selling to and serving in doesn't want them there, stop what you are doing and do something different. Immediately.

Knowing what to do is difficult on its own. Figuring out how your offering or product fits in an exceptionally saturated market is hard enough. But knowing what not to do and deciding on strategies to not do those things is often harder and often overlooked. Does your company have bloated and out-of-touch P&L methods? Stop using them. Change the method. Does your leadership disregard the inputs and valuable insights of the worker bees who know what the hell is going on? Listen to those people, and gain value from the knowledge *they* gained from their pain and experience in the profession. Is your leadership not reading the room and paying attention to indications from the community and leaders in your space that their offering is not well received and, in some cases, is being probed by people who make their living finding weaknesses in systems? Don't continue down that path. If you want to grow your business smartly and be the best leader you can be, you should take a minute and ask yourself, "What shouldn't we do?" It may be the most valuable question you ever ask.

CHAPTER

2

The Only Currencies That Matter as a Leader

Time

> Time is money, and I'll say it again . . . if someone is wasting
> your time, they are stealing from you. Wise up!
>
> —Kris Degioia

Leaders often need to give more credit to the currencies that are necessary to be most effective. Most of the literature in the space around leadership talks about the currency of leadership. But it's not one thing. No single currency will make you either a good or bad leader. And I'm not talking about the currency of money, to be precise. I'm talking in particular about the currencies of trust, time, and respect, which should be part of your piggy bank as a leader. You need to pay attention to them. If you ignore the criticality of the necessity and interaction of these currencies, which are fundamental to leadership, you are bankrupting your organization and, ultimately, yourself.

Being in a leadership position means those who work for and with you are invested in you with their most critical currency: time. That one currency is something no one can ever get back. Once it is spent, it is gone. Your employees and coworkers are investing their most valuable resource and their most fragile currency in you because they believe you will do something that will benefit them.

People don't come to work for you because they think you're terrific, they believe you're good-looking, or they think you smell nice. They won't stay up nights, spend time away from their families, and travel internationally because they want you to do better. They will do these things and sacrifice that most critical resource, time, for you because they believe there will be a payout for them. That's why we're all doing what we do: for a payout.

A payout isn't necessarily a cash windfall, although that is a real possibility for many employees in the technology space. If we're fortunate, we work for a leader who can grow a company, and an exit occurs, and everyone gets their share of the pie. That's great, but there are different types of payouts. A payout might be something as simple as a career opportunity, personal or professional growth, or the ability to climb the ladder into a different social class based on a job. Essentially, anything that you can offer someone that will make their life better is a payout.

Getting that payout is why someone comes to work for your company. They see that there's an opportunity for them to get some wins. Human beings prefer to avoid investing their most critical currency, time, into things where there is no chance of a payout; and if there is no upward mobility, financial growth, personal growth, or other payout, employees who give a damn about themselves will leave. *Some* employees *will* stay with a company for 40 years just because they like to have a warm place to sit their ass down and do a job. Still, in today's world, especially in a technology space like cybersecurity, most employees are otherwise motivated and looking for some form of benefit. So if we step back from that and understand that employees are working with and for us because they expect a payout, we can see that they are investing in us, and we owe them a substantial return on that investment.

Those who work with and for us invest that most valuable commodity, time, in our vision as leaders. They are taking time away from family, friends, and life that they will never get back. Every day spent commuting hours to work, every minute spent in a meeting they didn't want to be in and get no value from, every second they're on a call with the leader acting like a jerk, means hours of their lives are falling like sand through an hourglass. Most of us don't sit down and realize that we are operating on a clock. We all have only a certain number of ticks on that clock, and as each one ticks by, that's one less in the bank. As a leader, you must realize that you need to operationalize and optimize your employees' use of their time at all costs; if you don't do that, you are taking away their time on planet Earth.

Often, if you look at what you're doing and why those time thefts are occurring, it's not for the best reasons. Do you force your employees to engage in mandatory fun? Are you mandating that your employees show up at a function? Are you pushing your employees to commute to work because you invested in high-profile real estate that you think looks nice or that your investors enjoy, when they could just as efficiently work from home? Are you sending your employees emails on weekends when they should be spending time with family and friends? Are you treating your employees' time as less valuable than your own? As a leader, if you're doing any of those things, you are pillaging your employees' time on planet Earth, and you should reevaluate why you are doing what you are doing. Sooner or later, those employees will realize that there is time theft going on. And if the payout you are offering as their employer or leader is insufficient to compensate for their investment of time, you will burn that resource, and they will leave. Rightfully so.

Most people in the technology space who find themselves in leadership positions, especially new founders who do not have years of learning and managerial skills, need to consider the value proposition of time to employees. Here's an example from my personal experience. I do a lot of consulting with organizations from Silicon Valley, an area noted for amazing innovation that is usually synonymous with less-than-optimal business practices. In Silicon Valley, businesses typically have well-stocked kitchens and break areas combined with lavish benefit packages. Those benefits are great, as they incentivize employees to join the company. Still, in Silicon Valley, those jobs also require that people live in an area that is one of the most expensive in the United States. Those employees will also spend hours of their life commuting to that place of business.

Additionally, many Silicon Valley companies push their employees hard to participate in "family" events. Some of these things are fun, and some of them are fascinating, sure. And yes, there can be value in bringing your employees along to grow esprit de corps. But there's a fine line to walk. I have witnessed Silicon Valley companies push for mandatory fun events. While their employees grin and smile and act like they're having a good time, in truth, none of them want to be there, or they might want to be there for a little while and then go home. After all, they've already spent hours of their day commuting to get to that office, and they will spend hours commuting to get home, and they will do it all again the next day. It is rare for anyone to ask, "Why are we doing this?" or to stand up to the leadership of an organization and say, "Do you want to be here?" Typically, the leaders of these organizations take it as a given that their employees are so enamored with the opportunity to do something fun with no monetary outlay that they relish their participation in the event. All the while, their employees are thinking about a thousand things they would rather be doing at that moment.

The last time I was In Silicon Valley and participated in one of these mandatory fun events, it was like watching an episode of *The Walking Dead*. The event was scheduled during the annual RSA Cybersecurity Conference in San Francisco and was hosted in the company's offices. It was the typical type of event where food and drinks were provided, and all of the company's "local" employees were "invited" to attend. The founder did everything they could to make it an engaging and exciting event. But the smiles were pasted on. The founder and the leadership team didn't understand that the team was already burned out due to the preparations for the company's participation in the RSA event, working at breakneck speed for at least a month preparing for the annual parade of cybersecurity vendors. Engagement and enjoyment of the evening only lasted about 20 minutes before people were so tired that the energy was sucked out of the room. Those tired individuals were also drinking the alcohol provided freely, which only complicated things and further brought down the mood in the space. They were either drunk, sleeping, or staggering around the room, waiting for 8:00 so they could leave and go home, trying to keep it together, blinking at the time, and wishing the seconds would move faster. It was not a good look for the founder, and it was not a good look for the company. No leads or potential deals came from this engagement.

Having been to and participated in hundreds of these events, I have seen this exact scenario play out over and over. While this might not be front-page news, it's still a relevant point to consider. Food and drinks and music sounds like a great time. And maybe it is. But when the leadership does not consider the time the employees have already spent preparing for a significant event and then adds a mandatory fun operation, it never plays out well—the lack of engagement and disinterest ooze into the space. And the founders and leadership team only come off looking like inconsiderate jerks whose employees couldn't care less about engaging with potential customers and clients.

Recent research published on the importance of time provides additional insight into its value as a currency. In a study published by the University of Pennsylvania and UCLA, the researchers asked a primary series of questions, such as "What would you rather have, more time or money?" Most people gave the typically expected practical answer: around 64 percent surveyed answered "more money." But the study also discovered something else. The people who said they'd prefer more time specifically noted being happier and more fulfilled in life. This relationship between happiness and time also held when the researchers controlled for the participants' time and money in their response criteria.

Time as a benefit for a person is not as obviously understood as "I want more of both." The truth is much more subtle. What matters is the value people place on a resource. "Beyond the amount of these resources people *have*, happiness is linked to the resource people *want*" (Hershfield, 2016). Logic suggests that anyone will want both more time and more money. But unfortunately, there is rarely an opportunity to gain both simultaneously.

Life is a series of trade-offs between resources. Time is the only truly finite resource; anyone can make more money. You can take someone's money, and it is not that final, but taking their time is the ultimate act of selfishness. We are all operating on a clock, and by taking someone's valuable time for less than truly practical reasons, you are taking from their happiness and satisfaction. Do you want unhappy, unsatisfied employees representing your company? I hope not.

Does this mean your organization should never have fun events for employees? Are you stealing someone's time simply by having an after-work event? On the other hand, will it hinder your business's growth if you are *not* engaging in after-hours events with customers and clients? There's not a single solid answer to those questions. Your organization and its leadership should be exceptionally cautious about how you approach those endeavors. The best way to think about it is to conduct a cost-versus-benefit analysis based on your employees' time. Statistically, data suggests that most after-hours events with customers and clients yield a rate of return of less than 5 percent on future deals. It might be worth it to your organization; 5 percent of a $10 million contract is a nice chunk of change. The point is not to say "Don't have those after-hours events"; nor is it to say that you shouldn't engage your employees outside of working hours. The point is that time is a finite resource that your employees, customers, and clients are constantly concerned about. Make sure your organization's leaders seriously consider the impact and value of any event or action that requires someone else's time. It's that simple. If you are considerate of this most valuable resource, your organization, your business, your employees, and your customers and clients will ultimately benefit.

Trust

> The best way to find out if you can trust somebody is to trust them.
>
> Ernest Hemingway

Trust is one of the most foundational concepts and principles our species has leveraged throughout our journey out of the primordial muck. Consider that when a baby is born, it is different from every other animal on the planet in that a human baby cannot,

within hours of birth, move or have any chance of survival outside the mother. Other animals are born and instinctively know
they must be mobile to make it to day two. Humans are born
prematurely. We aren't fully formed and functional before our
oversized brains and egg-shaped heads rocket through the birth
canal. Because of our large brains, humans are "smarter" at birth
than other animals, but we depend entirely on adults to keep us
alive for at least our first few years on Earth. We survive by trusting our parents and others who care for us, and we have been
doing so for eons. Trust is necessary for our early survival and is
hardwired to our deepest evolutionary needs. Trust is not a luxury.

The first cave people had to base their decision-making on
trust. They had to trust that whomever they chose as their leader
would find them food, shelter, and safety. It was incumbent on
that leader to take care of their clan and ensure that bellies were
full and predators were kept at bay. Since the dawn of time,
humanity has used trust and the perception of a trustworthy
leader as guiding principles. Fail to provide food on the regular,
Grog? We don't trust you. Rock-and-stick attacks ensue, and
Grog is replaced with a new, more perceivably trustworthy provider. Back down and run away when the wolves are at the cave
mouth, Ook? Be gone. The brood will find a braver, more
dependable, more decisive leader.

As we evolved, even our brain chemistry changed to make
trusting another person a good thing. Various research shows
that the brain chemistry that governs our emotions also plays a
role in trust. Paul Zak, a researcher in the new field of neuroeco-
nomics, demonstrated that oxytocin, a powerful chemical found
in our bodies, can boost feelings of trust between people. Other
research shows how intimately oxytocin relates to a person's positive emotional state.

Animals become calmer, more sedate, and less anxious when
injected with oxytocin. Increased oxytocin levels are also found

in the brain after a person establishes a successful social connection. We are chemically driven to seek beneficial trust relationships because our brains "like" the feeling we get when that positive, affirming connection happens.

When we trust something or someone, it feels good. To be clear, I don't mean you should spend your time as a leader trying to jack up your employees' oxytocin levels. I mean that you should work to genuinely imbue them with those good chemicals via your actions. If you generate trust and your employees trust you, then you can expect that chemical boost, and that is a good thing. Conversely, if you reduce that critical feeling of trust, you should expect fewer happy chemicals and, ultimately, fewer happy, trustful employees.

Trust affects our physical interactions and social connections; trust-related decisions are considerable inputs on which we base our decision-making. Consider the social interactions you have on a personal level. Have you ever had a bad handshake? How did that affect your immediate consideration of how much trust you would put in that person? Doesn't a less-than-genuine smile or hug call a person's intentions into question? The ability of a person to establish a direct trust relationship with you can come from something as benign as that one short physical interaction. If that interaction does not connect with your deeply human Spidey sense of trust, that relationship is already at risk. We seek to know how we should trust everyone we interact with in various ways, all of which are traceable back to the day we were born and first looked up at our mothers with those big doe eyes.

If we do not perceive that trust is present or feel that trust is warranted, our whole interaction with that potentially untrustworthy individual is suspect. Trust is a currency that is constantly exchanged. Most people will trust you if you trust them or give them a reason to. Trust is intuitive and, like any sound currency, can be earned and invested. If your employees, partners, and even customers feel like you trust them, they will impart their trust to you, work harder and smarter, or invest in your service or product. Mutual trust breeds respect, which we will discuss later as the ultimate currency; but know that without trust, there will never be respect, and vice versa.

Building, managing, and growing trust must be a key focus for everyone in the company. From the CEO to every employee in the organization, trust must be a core behavior. Good leaders trust their managers to engage and drive their teams, and managers must trust their teams to be productive and communicate honestly.

To help build that critical trust in your company, you must work on these practices:

- Listen authentically whenever possible. Put the phone down, look your people in the eye, and genuinely listen to them.

- Practice integrity. Never approach things as "Do as I say, not as I do." Integrity must always be present and part of your communications and daily lives.

- Communicate openly. Be honest with your staff, speak candidly, and explain the rationale behind decisions. Make sure everyone understands the why, not just the how.

- Have humility. Be prepared to admit mistakes and say when you don't have the answer. But never be satisfied with "I don't know" as an answer. Find the answer, and ask others to do the same.

- Put people first. Work to keep your team and everyone engaged and satisfied.

- Get ahead of personnel problems and see them to their resolution.

- Demonstrate empathy. Put yourself in others' shoes. Take the time to reflect on why someone did something and understand their positions on things that matter to them.

A solid foundation of trust that permeates your organization will save you and your employees when things go wrong. Which they will. When things go sideways is not the time to try to build a relationship of trust with your people. If that trust is not already present when things get tough and difficult days lie ahead, things will undoubtedly crumble in your organization.

A great example of failing to build trust within a team came when I was literally inside a burning building.

Let me explain. In the Navy, firefighting is everyone's responsibility. A fire at sea is the worst thing to happen to a ship. When you are in the middle of the ocean and a fire breaks out, no fire department is coming to save you, and if you cannot put the fire out, it's a long swim home. To prepare the crew for this possibility, the Navy sends all sailors through basic firefighting training in boot camp. Those who desire a bit more of an adrenaline rush can volunteer to attend advanced firefighting school: 80 hours of real-world firefighting. And by real-world, I mean you are put in your firefighting gear and dumped into a five-story building that is on fire from the floor to the ceiling. That fire *is* controlled by computers and fed by natural gas, limiting the risk of real harm.

Nonetheless, it's a building on fire. It is a gauntlet. The training is a hot, stinky, sweaty, smoky, terrifying gauntlet lasting eight hours a day for two weeks. When sailors attend this school, they will get about a year of firefighting training in two weeks. If the phrase "drinking from the fire hose" was ever applicable, it is at Navy Advanced Firefighting School.

When I attended this school, we were preparing for a six-month deployment to the Persian Gulf. My team had been through the primary firefighting school at boot camp and had attended several scenario-based training events to prepare us for this operation. But we had never been in the mix like this, and none of us had ever been locked in the dark, sweating like rats in a wool sock, starved of oxygen, and staring an inferno in the face.

We had a great deal of training and should have been prepared—but until you face the monster, it's all just concept.

My team could have fared better on the first day. We made it about 10 feet into the inferno, and everyone at the back of the fire team got hot, ran out of easy air, and bailed. That abandonment left me, our team leader, and my number-one nozzleman standing feet from the blaze with no backup. To put it mildly, our trust in our compatriots was lacking after that event.

Fast-forward two days into the training, and we still had not made it past the third floor of the "hot box."

Each time we made progress, someone on the team would run, panting and flailing, out of the building. As that person left, the next would follow, and if those of us at the front of the hose were lucky, two to three would remain in the fight until the instructors shut us down and summarily ejected us from the building. Because of our failure and lack of execution, the team would then be "smoked," which meant made to do push-ups and jumping jacks in full gear (masks on) until someone puked or we just fell out. It was July in Norfolk, Virginia, where the air was thick with salt and the haze of ship diesel fuel, which only furthered our breathing problems and made each exercise seem to stretch onward into eternity. Men dropped like flies, helmets were vomited into, and generally, it sucked.

It wasn't until day four, during a break in the last smoke session of the first week, that my team leader directly asked, "Who is afraid of fire? Who is afraid of closed spaces? Who is afraid of the dark? Who is going to bail when they can't breathe?" Two hands went up. "Okay, good. You two are excused. Go back to the ship." And with that, those sailors left. We spent the rest of our break time talking as a unit and asking each member what else they needed to stay in the fight. Our leader had a very frank conversation with the fire team and ensured that everyone trusted one another to hang on until the end of each scenario. Each of us was open about our fears and individual motivations for being there. Each team member looked one another in the eye and said honestly, "I will not leave."

The remaining team members also asked the instructors for a training break where we could "prove" our equipment. We meant that we wanted to walk through the scenario without the full firefighting ensemble. Even though we had been using our gear for days and no one had been injured or burned, we needed to prove to ourselves that we could function in the heavy, cumbersome ensembles. And we needed to see each other physically maneuver through the space in our full kit. Observing one another before the space became a raging inferno would aid our decision-making and help us prove to ourselves that we could move, breathe, and function in the dark. We conducted several dry runs in a variety of different kits to increase our training and familiarize us with the actions we would need to take. We started with no gear on and no fire and practiced, each time increasing the adoption of gear, and finally donning our full ensemble and lighting the building aflame. Those practice sessions also made us more familiar with the internals of the space. By doing those dry runs without our gear, we also realized that we were substantially better off with our gear on. With the ensemble on, we had limited peripheral vision, but our forward vision was optimized; and in our ensembles, we had lights on our helmets that would pierce smoke and the darkness. Thanks to the heat and lack of atmospheric air movement, we were still struggling for air in the training space even without SCBA tanks on, but we continued our practice repeatedly, each time working through the fear and angst of the lack of air. We became familiar, if not somewhat comfortable, with the constant lack of oxygen. Once we had walked the space without the masks on and with no positive airflow, the team knew that even though the masks were stifling, constant air was better than sucking wind with no oxygen supply.

Finally, we practiced moving the water hose around the space without the ensemble on and noted that the weight and roughness of the hose caused painful abrasions on our skin. With no thick firefighting gloves, everything was hot and pain-inducing. That session helped us have more trust in our gear and trust in the need for that ensemble to keep us alive even when we were in a space engulfed in flames.

The fire team was down a few members. Still, thanks to an honest series of questions and all of us, including our leadership, having the integrity to admit we were afraid of what we were doing, we were better off. Even with a reduced force, we were functionally better. By the morning of day five, we made it to the top of the building and were doing fine with our training. No one else would back out and leave on the team, and our ability to operate and do the job increased exponentially. We trusted each other to stay in the fight, recognized our shared issues and fears, and faced them as a unit.

Did we suddenly get better simply because we got rid of the weak links? No, not really. Being afraid of fire and dark and small spaces is normal. Any human with a semblance of self-preservation instinct does not desire to stare at a blazing inferno. It is natural to be afraid, but trusting your teammates and each other's commitment to the mission is vital. We were more successful because we had built up the trust needed so that no one would abandon the team; those who remained wanted to be there, and they would stay in the fight. It didn't matter that none of us could understand why those other sailors had volunteered for this detail. Why anyone would want to be in on something like this when they knew they were fearful of it was beyond us, but at least now we knew that those who remained were on the team for the right reasons. Our communications were better, as the team had more trust in one another's answers and commands. And thanks to the practice and our shared trust in one another, when a real fire did happen at sea, our team responded flawlessly, and no one had to swim home.

Establishing trust can be the difference between life and death. Had we not prepared and tested our trust in one another, things would have gone far worse when the actual fire happened at sea. If we were not trusting of one another's ability, bravery, knowledge, and skills when a real fire occurred, someone, perhaps many, would have died. Establishing trust must happen before things get dicey, and if that trust relationship is strong enough, your organization can stare the blaze in the face and move forward smoothly. Do not wait to establish trust.

Invest time and energy in building trust, the most valuable currency when a crisis strikes. A strong foundation of trust allows a culture of resiliency, accountability, and problem-solving to flourish, enabling your business to endure, or even thrive, in the most brutal storms. And what's more, you don't have to know what's coming to focus on building trust right now.

Respect

Respect is a two-way street, if you want to get it, you've got to give it.

R.G. Risch

The irony of leading a company or managing people is that the people who desire or overtly seek to be in a leadership position tend not to be good leaders. These individuals are typically cut from similar cloth. They are usually extroverts who like to control things. Those things might be people, family, events, calendars, or any other potentially controllable aspect of daily life. In short, they are usually control freaks. And a control freak does not a good leader make. Conversely, many people throughout history who are considered great leaders never sought out formal power.

They never wanted to be leaders; it was thrust upon them. The best leaders are reluctant ones. They are those rare people who are hesitant to leverage their positional authority unless it is absolutely necessary. These individuals do not relish the power of authority; they genuinely desire only to help others succeed. They constantly focus on their core values as part of their leadership style—values like integrity, humility, service above self, and thoughtfulness, which are essential values for any great leader. That authenticity and lack of overt authoritarianism, not social dominance or positional authority, help them gain respect.

There are many ways to commit leadership suicide, but perhaps one of the most repeated by young or inexperienced managers is confusing their own personal desire to be liked by everyone with a leader's need to be respected. No manager can succeed in leading people if they are disliked or feared. The days of military-style leadership in the workplace are well behind us. However, seeking popularity as a leader is just as prone to failure, as it is a sign of weakness. In the short term, you will be popular; but in the long term, when hard decisions are required, you will fail.

If the currency of leadership were popularity, leaders would avoid difficult decisions and uncomfortable conversations. And when they did engage in those issues, their ability to be effective would be clouded by their need to be popular or liked. As a leader, you have to get your team to want to follow you. That desire will not come from being popular—you don't have to be everyone's best friend—but that doesn't mean you have to be a jerk, either. Wanting to follow you will come from your employees and others seeing you as a respect-worthy, fair, and effective person.

If popularity is a false currency for leaders, so is power. Leaders cannot force people to cooperate, and a good leader does not try to replace democracy with dictatorship. Leaders with no followers are not leaders. They are lonely figureheads marching along to the drum beat of their own idiocy. The ultimate victory of a leader is when influence is gained, which is achieved over time by seeking and giving respect.

A leader can help themselves earn respect by creating positive challenges. People want to follow others who have vision and ambition. People seek out those who have their eyes on the prize and are willing to work to help that person achieve their dream. Inside most of us is a burning desire to make a difference, so tapping into this ambition is powerful for a leader. People are more inspired when they are working toward creating great things. "Everyone likes a winner" is a very valid phrase. However, when a leader stretches people and pushes them to aim high, that leader must, of course, support those employees and those goals to make it a positive challenge. By setting stretch goals that are likely not to be achieved and by not supporting the people and processes working to achieve that goal, a leader shows that they are undeserving of respect and trust. This is a deadly combination for anyone in a leadership position.

Let me give you the best example of how losing your employees' respect can erode your leadership effectiveness. This story comes from an interaction with a client I was consulting for. I can't use actual names in this story, but trust me, I would like to. So, for the purposes of this narrative, I will simply call the leader Dick (because that's what he was, and likely still is as a person, to be honest).

The company I was consulting for was doing well. It was growing better than expected compared to most others in the market. This company had already been in the market for over two decades and had recently maneuvered into position for a future acquisition. The numbers and growth trajectory were on pace, but the sales efforts were beginning to stall out a bit for various reasons. Not the least of these was the lack of investment in the company's marketing efforts and the focus of the outreach program. As it stood, the marketing efforts weren't much more than updates to the website, the occasional social media post, and the always necessary (but minimally useful) outreach to the big analyst firms. It was a haphazard approach to establishing the company brand and marketing the organization in a very crowded and competitive space. While efforts were underway to help establish the company as a dominant market force, the real focus was on sales, sales, and more sales.

Logically, this made sense, as the company was not aiming to take on any outside capital, and the opportunity for growth was certainly there. But Dick was solely focused on keeping the sales numbers climbing as the only metric that mattered and was hell-bent on ensuring that growth occurred "by any means necessary." Dick's focus was based on his past experience at other companies where he had been integral in company acquisitions and on his market research. For him, the magical rule of 40 was the only driver the company should focus on. The rule of 40 is the principle, mainly used by venture capital firms, that a software company's combined growth rate and profit margin should exceed 40 percent. In simpler terms, if your company is not growing at 40 percent year over year, nothing else matters. While that might be a good benchmark and a useful one for Software as a Service (SaaS) companies, it is not a biblical standard or a number marked in stone somewhere. But Dick could not see any other way of measuring the company or its employees' effectiveness aside from the rule of 40. If the company was not growing north of 40 percent, regardless of marketing or investment, or employee input, or anything else, it was a total fail.

Dick was tied to this number as "the industry standard and the only way to prove a value," and if that growth was not visible at each week's sales call, he would unleash his wrath on whoever was on the call. And by his wrath, I mean his actual wrath. Dick would start a call and show the numbers the sales teams had provided him. As soon as the metric dipped below

40 percent growth, the monster would come out. For Dick, his monster would raise its voice, not enough to be reported to HR for screaming, but enough that no one else could talk over or to him. His anger would seethe out from every pore on his face and permeate the entire call. The team would sit in stunned silence, waiting for their flogging like elementary students outside the head nun's office. Heads hung, eyes down and darting, the team simply waited for his rants and accusations to end so they could get off the call and go back to hustling to try to get the company more dollars in the door. Dick was so adamant about the need to be at 40 percent growth that he even prodded sales leaders to stack deals in forward quarters and reports to keep the numbers "solid." Anyone who challenged Dick was as good as dead at the company. His wrath was the only thing that was expected each week. There was no good news, and the team would never want to succeed for any reason other than to get Dick to shut up. And Dick was the CEO! He ran the entire company this way.

During one particularly unpleasant call with his team—and I use the term "team" loosely, as there was no more team present than Knights Templars at the Alamo—I saw an opportunity to try to interrupt Dick's rage rant. Bad idea. The entire sales team and all the executive leadership were on this call, and things were about to go completely off the rails.

Dick: (Speaking with the tone of an older, angrier sibling, eyes drawn tight, and fist thumping his desk) We aren't going to hit our goals this quarter. Someone tell me why this keeps happening. We have been running at the right rate for months now, and we have had the biggest year for the company in decades, and we haven't changed anything. So, what's wrong here? I don't want to hear your excuses. I want answers.

No one responded. The faces of everyone on the Zoom call were hollow and zombie-like. Everyone could feel the temperature increasing. Visible sweat was present on at least a few of the team members' foreheads.

Dick: (Louder now, tone terse, eyes wide open, fist pounding on his desk, face red) I am asking a simple question. Why are we slowing down, and why aren't you lining up deals? Our pipeline is abysmal.

I decided to chime in.

Me: Well, Dick, if I were still at the analyst firm you contracted me away from, this is where I would tell you that this company is basically at stall speed. The sales and leadership team have done all they can with what they have, and they are now at the tipping point. Either something does change, like taking an investment or starting to put more money, real money, into marketing, or this is what you should expect. The numbers are not a result of anyone on this call not hustling, but no money has been allocated to marketing or even operations. I don't see how anyone is actually selling anything with the way things are running. You have allocated no investment in anything to grow the business. And mathematically, there is no way to keep the prior pace of wins up unless something changes.

Dick: (Head back, hands waving, visibly upset, leaning into the webcam) I just said I don't want excuses. If it was working before, it should work now. This is not a forum for strategy discussions. We need tactical execution and sales. Stop with the excuses.

Me: None of what I just said is an excuse. That was an explanation; there is a difference. Those are the facts. This is why companies in this space take on investment to grow. You can eat what you kill for only so long in this space. And as you pointed out, the abysmal leads list is a result of weak marketing, not a lack of effort. No matter how hard you squeeze, you can't get blood from a stone.

Dick: More excuses (now with clear contempt and rage in his face and voice, fist pounding on the desk). I am sick of the lack of execution of this team, and the only thing that might change around here is getting rid of the dead weight if you people can't sell this product.

Me: So, just to be clear, you, as the CEO, expect your sales and leadership team to sell more and execute better with no logistical or financial support? And you think it's valuable to speak to grown adults like they are your children?

Dick abruptly kicked me off the sales call. My Zoom login was terminated, and I was removed from future invites to the team meetings. Fine by me, if I am honest. No one wanted to be on those calls with him, and I felt fortunate to have an easy out. But I felt terrible for the poor souls left on that call. I pictured them all looking forlorn and waiting for Dick's tirade to end.

But what about the respect piece of this? Dick had shown his true colors. He was a bully. And not a good one. Dick was a keyboard warrior of the highest order. Dick had shown that he would rage when he was behind the camera and safely tucked away in his home office, but when confronted, he folded like a cardboard box in a hurricane. He was fine being the overbearing asshole who placed the blame for the company stalling out on everyone but him. Like any bully, his cowardice came out the moment he was challenged. Even though he had been presented with facts that proved where things were going wrong, and regardless of his own failures, Dick was unwilling to admit that the fault lay entirely with him.

What Dick didn't know was that as soon as I was kicked off the Zoom call, my phone blew up with text messages. Every member of the team that I had some relationship with gave me the play-by-play of what happened after I was ousted.

Having seen the bully falter and take the easy way out of removing a valid challenge to his authority, the team watched as Dick went further down the rabbit hole of blame and shame. Following my removal, Dick simply caved in on himself and wavered between screaming and fits of "Why me?" Dick's authority as a CEO and respect investment ebbed out of the call like water out of a leaky bucket. By losing his temper, avoiding valid challenges, and chastising everyone who was doing their job, Dick had destroyed his flimsy hold as a leader. He was respectless and without any means to regain that valuable lost currency.

No one wants to be bullied. And when you are leading an organization, losing your temper and blaming the people doing the work is the surest, quickest way to lose their respect. Now what was Dick to do? How could he expect things to change when the team that was going to do the desperately needed work felt only one of two ways towards him: afraid or contemptuous? Dick's fit and the ensuing lack of respect his team members felt guaranteed that the stall the company was facing would soon turn into a crash. And that is just what happened. Over the next quarter, the company sales pipeline dried up, sales growth hit a plateau, and the board started asking very serious questions about whether Dick was the right person to be CEO. Obviously, the answer to that question was no.

While a leader's position often comes with a degree of inherent respect, that respect can't and won't sustain itself for an extended period. It is a currency that does not grow on its own. Respect is an investment account that you must continually pay into to receive any future return. Respect is earned, and it's earned through a lot of hard work, cautious decision-making, and calm, respectful interactions with the team. As Paulo Coelho said, "Respect is for those who deserve it, not for those who demand it." Once respect is lost, gaining it back is one of the hardest things a leader can do. According to a variety of research, respect is noted as one of the most important traits a leader must maintain:

- In a survey conducted by *Harvard Business Review*, 72 percent of respondents said that respect was the most important leadership behavior to them, more than any other behavior (Goffee, 2017).

- A study published in the *Journal of Applied Psychology* found that when employees felt respected by their supervisors, they were more likely to feel committed to their organization and less likely to experience burnout (Group, 2018).

- Another study published in the *Journal of Management* found that leaders who showed respect to their employees had higher job satisfaction, commitment, and engagement levels among their team members (Johnson, 2014).

- In a survey of 20,000 employees, the Boston Consulting Group found that the most important leadership behavior that employees wanted to see was "respect for my opinions and ideas" (Porath, 2007).

- In a study conducted by the Society for Human Resource Management, 65 percent of employees said that respect was a very important factor in their job satisfaction, and 72 percent said that their immediate supervisor's respect for them was important to their job satisfaction (Society for Human Resource Management, 2016).

As you can guess from the earlier narrative and the data and sources I have cited, respect is critical. As a leader, you must maintain a level of respect, but you do so by giving respect first. You do not command respect. Well, you can try, but you won't get respect. If anything, you will get fear, discontent, and fake smiles. But you won't be respected, and ultimately, people's lack of respect will show up. That empty respect bank will affect your ability to execute.

The Most Valuable Currency

Time, trust, and respect are three of the most fundamentally valuable currencies any leader must have in their bank. None of these three characteristics is necessarily more valuable than any other. And none of these three characteristics should exist in a vacuum. My research indicates that, when asked, most employees say the

As a leader, what is the most valuable "currency" you can have with your organization?

You can see how people vote. **Learn more**

Respect ✓   7%

Trust   83%

Time (respecting people's time)   5%

Other (please comment)   4%

206 votes • Poll closed • **Remove vote**

FIGURE 2.1 A short research poll conducted by Dr. Chase Cunningham detailing the most valuable leadership currency

most important trait for a leader is their ability to be trusted. (See Figure 2.1.) But how do you gain that trust? You gain that trust by engaging in things such as two-way respect, valuing the employees' time, and trusting your people to do the right thing.

To grow any of those currencies requires you to be somewhat uncomfortable. To gain trust, you must trust. To gain respect, you must offer respect to people you might not think deserve it. To value others' time, you must value your own time. If your goal is to be a good leader and not be a "Dick," you must continually consider how your behavior and your attitude either invest or divest in these critical character traits.

CHAPTER

3

You Deserve What You Tolerate

You get what you expect, and you deserve what you tolerate.
—Mark Graban

The first horse I ever rode bucked me off after about 30 seconds. We made it maybe a quarter of a mile from the barn when the horse suddenly decided he'd had enough and wanted to go home. I was about nine at the time and already terrified of sitting on the back of 1,000 pounds of muscle and hair. But it was interesting, and every kid wants to ride a horse, right? This horse had a reputation for being somewhat ornery and was known to make his own decisions. However, he was a smaller horse, and I was a young guy, so they put me on the back of this monster. We left the barn, got outside the paddock, and were making our way up the trail when this horse (I think his name was Black Ant) began to turn his head and look back at the barn. The horse had figured out that he was larger than me, stronger than me, and, most important, more motivated than I was to not be on a ride that day. The further we walked, the more head jerking the horse did, which soon turned into an abrupt about-face. Once he could see the barn, nothing I did mattered. The horse could see the promised land and knew all he had to do was remove the annoying human on his back, get to the barn, and his life would be good. The horse took a few big steps, reared up as high as he could, landed back on all fours, and vaulted me into the stratosphere before trotting away. Obviously, this was less than ideal for me. It not only hurt my pride but also negated any future claim I had to being a valuable cowboy. Luckily, I wasn't badly damaged when I bounced to the ground. The worst part was that after being hip-tossed by a horse, I had to walk back to the barn with my head low to retrieve the animal. It was one of the most embarrassing and shameful moments of my young life.

After returning to the barn and finding the horse in his stall, munching on grass and enjoying his leftover oats, it was my task to figure out how the hell to get him back out into the paddock and, ultimately, onto the trail. I was terrified, to say the least. I had experienced the unrestrained power of this beast. He had let me know he was in charge and could do whatever he wanted whenever he wanted. As I walked up to the horse and grabbed his bridle, he gave me a side eye and a hard snort. He stomped his front feet. And he shook his head violently to let me know this wasn't a fight I wanted or could win. And what was I to do? Somehow, this herbivore had figured out that he was the dominant force and that the laws of physics were in his favor. Not only that, but he'd also realized that he could intimidate me. For the moment, I could only stand there holding his bridle and hoping he didn't bite or kick me while I tried to figure out an excuse to leave.

It was about this time when the head wrangler, a wonderful young lady named Sarah, rode up and asked me what was going on. She knew exactly what was going on because she had seen the entire fiasco, but she was kind enough to let me explain what occurred. With tear-filled eyes, I told her I did not know what to do, I was afraid of the horse, and I wasn't sure I could ride this animal anymore. I also told her I was embarrassed to go back out in front of the other people. Sarah, being the awesome person she was, simply sat in her saddle and shrugged her shoulders before asking me an eye-opening question: "Do you think I'm stronger than this horse?" Sarah raised her eyebrow as she asked me, "Do you think I haven't been bucked off and kicked and bitten by this horse? Because I have. I have been just as embarrassed as you are right now, and I know it's not easy to get back in the saddle. But I also know you deserve what you tolerate when it comes to horses. If you allow this animal to be your boss, that's exactly what will happen. He's smart. But he's an animal. And he's been ridden plenty by a lot of people who are smaller than you. If you allow him to think he's in charge, and you don't take command, you should expect to get bucked off and keep walking back to the barn. Or you can jump back in that saddle, take a breath, and take charge of that horse. He's smart. And part of being smart means he doesn't like discomfort. Use his bit and your weight to let him know you mean business. If you're in charge and keep his head pointed forward, he'll come around."

I wish I could tell you that, like in a Hollywood movie, I jumped back on the horse and took perfect command of him, and we had an amazing day. But that's not what happened. I did jump back on the horse, and I did my best to take command, but he bucked me off two more times. I did not let up. Even though the horse was winning and I was getting more bruised as the day went on, I wasn't going to let him be in charge. He was a smart horse. After kicking my ass a few times, he figured out this little human wasn't going away. He was also tired of having his bridle jerked and his ribs kicked. So he relented, and we eventually went on a decent ride together.

Why am I telling you a story about a horse, other than to cement the belief that I was never meant to be a cowboy? Now that I'm writing this book and retelling some of these stories, I realize I wasn't a very good cowboy. It was probably best for my own safety that I joined the Navy and left the farm. Anyway, I'm telling you this story because I deserved exactly what I was tolerating with this animal. I am not comparing people to animals, although we've all met some humans who probably belong in the animal kingdom. The point I'm trying to make is that we often fail to realize we are allowing, encouraging, and tolerating the very behaviors we know are detrimental to success.

Most of us had parents or guardians who did their best to provide us with a solid foundation for life. Part of their job as parents was to teach us the difference between right and wrong, moral and immoral, and legal and illegal. Thanks to our parents or other mentors, we learned the basics of what is and isn't acceptable, what they would tolerate from us, and what we should tolerate from others.

We should have learned when to stop tolerating and start acting. It's a hard leap to make, but it's critical to act once an unwanted action or behavior is identified. Most people know what is acceptable and what is unacceptable but are unwilling to act when confronted with the need to correct unacceptable behavior. Some leaders are concerned about being perceived as the bad guy, and some just willingly pass the buck; they think it's not their job. Others simply don't like confrontation and avoid it at all costs.

The problem with those approaches is that the action or behavior never gets addressed, and failing to address it is the same as condoning it. Tolerating the negative is the same as endorsing it. As a leader, you don't have the option of looking the other way; it's your duty to act. The buck stops with you, or it will never stop.

What should you tolerate, and what should you confront? Are there any examples or behaviors you should immediately address when they rear their ugly heads? Yes, certainly. If you recall the story about Dick, you will remember how he focused on "not wanting excuses," which is logical. But Dick didn't really understand the differences and values between an explanation and an excuse, and that lack of understanding harmed his respect and trust investments. Let's delineate the differences between excuses and explanations and see why one is acceptable and possibly helpful and the other is a negative behavior to address quickly as a leader.

Imagine a salesperson who has consistently missed their sales target for several months in a row. When their manager asks them why they haven't met their target, the salesperson responds with an excuse such as "The market is just too competitive right now," "The economy is in a downturn, so customers aren't buying as much," "My dog ate my sample case," or "I have carpal tunnel, and it hurts to click a mouse." Those are all excuses; none of them are very good, and some are lame. But they are excuses, nonetheless. Okay, maybe not the carpal tunnel excuse, but you get the point.

The salesperson is making excuses for their poor performance instead of taking responsibility for it. Although it's true that external factors can affect sales performance, a leader who tolerates these types of excuses risk creating a culture of blame-shifting and underperformance. Other people on that salesperson's team will hear how the excuse was accepted or rejected and adapt their responses based on their understanding of that interaction. Excuses are a cancer for execution. Any accepted excuse plants the seeds of "Hey, I can get away with this!" in the minds of those who see an excuse as a viable response.

If a leader tolerates excuses, it will lead to a culture of mediocrity and lack of accountability. Failure becomes acceptable, and there are no consequences for not meeting expectations. This does not mean you must be a Dick when you hear an excuse. There is no value in going bonkers, but you should let it be known that what you heard was an excuse, and you don't tolerate excuses. You want an excuse to be a less-than-comfortable statement. You should also be aware that if you won't accept excuses, you should not make any of your own. If you do, you will lose your people's respect and trust. "Do as I say, not as I do" is never an acceptable leadership statement (Willink, 2017).

On the other hand, an explanation is a statement that clarifies or sheds light on a situation or event without trying to absolve people of responsibility or avoid accountability (Kruse, 2018). It provides context and information to help others understand the reasons behind a particular outcome, decision, or action. For example, "I wasn't able to attend the meeting because I had a family emergency" is an explanation: it provides context for why the person was absent without trying to avoid responsibility for missing the meeting.

When someone explains, they share their perspective on what happened, why it happened, and what they are doing to address it. This can help others make informed decisions and work together to find solutions to problems. An excuse is usually an emotive phrase followed by a "because" statement: for example, "I am afraid I won't hit my numbers this quarter. But it was because of the market, not my efforts." That's an excuse of the highest order.

An explanation often includes facts, dates, and truth (Kerr, 2019). Blaming the market for a lack of sales execution sounds like a data-driven statement, but it's only a means of using a fact to shift blame. If that statement were changed to an explanation, it would be more like, "I missed my target this quarter. Because the market in our vertical saw a 20 percent reduction in investment, my sales contacts have been reducing their spend for this quarter. I understand where they are coming from, but we are adjusting our pricing to attempt to entice more growth from those clients soon."

When you hear someone offering what is obviously an excuse, ask the person to explain it without any mention of blame or shifting of responsibility. You are asking the person making that excuse to stop, think, and change their response to a more thoughtful reply that is worth listening to. This will let others in the room or the team know that while you may hear an excuse, you won't be a belligerent ass and crucify whoever offered it. We all make excuses sometimes, but we want to listen to explanations instead. You are okay with a reasonable explanation for a failure; you see value in the knowledge gained from that hiccup in execution. You will tolerate an intelligent, fact-driven admission of failure. But you will not accept a cop-out that has no value for learning or addressing an obvious problem.

People tend to be more forgiving and understanding when someone provides an honest explanation for a mistake or failure, as opposed to making an excuse. By taking ownership of their actions and providing context for what happened, individuals can demonstrate that they are committed to learning from their mistakes and working collaboratively to improve outcomes in the future.

Another great life lesson about tolerating people's failures and behaviors came in the middle of the Persian Gulf at night, surrounded by potentially hostile threats. It was an uncomfortable time, to say the least.

During the early days of the Iraq war, in 2002, during the invasion, I was onboard the USS Cape St. George, a guided missile cruiser tasked with defending the aircraft carrier USS Dwight D. Eisenhower from hostile action. Added to that mission, our battle group was tasked with intercepting and repelling any potential water-borne threats. Usually, those were small boats or the odd Iranian Navy ship that happened to wander into our area of operations. My job at that time was as a member of the Visit, Board, Search, and Seizure (VBSS) team. This team's mission was to intercept any of those hostile water-borne threats and engage them if need be. Usually, that engagement was more of a standoff. The rogue boat usually saw us coming and turned around once they realized a US Navy team was on the way. In a few cases, they tried to navigate around us to get closer to the battle group, so we called on the destroyer in our group to fire off a few rounds and then watched the enemy vessel promptly haul ass back to their safe zone. For this to work, though, we had to have fully functional, small go-fast boats that could carry roughly 12 men and weapons at high speed to intercept threats. Those boats required maintenance to stay operational. That is where the story takes a turn.

The group responsible for our small-boat maintenance was the auxiliary team onboard the USS Cape St. George. These were trained technicians who were tasked with keeping the small boats operational, as well as any other auxiliary technology onboard the ship. The technician trained in small-boat upkeep was the problem child. I will call him Matt (not his real name). Matt was consistently lazy and hardly ever made an operation on time, the type of person who would be late for his own funeral. He displayed overt disrespectful behavior and had been in various physical and verbal altercations with the leadership in his sector. Finally, although he graduated from the school that trained technicians to do maintenance on the small boats, Matt was never around when things needed to be fixed. He ghosted the other technicians regularly for work in different work centers that he enjoyed more. Matt was also mentally absent from meetings; he showed up but was never engaged. His mind was always elsewhere. Finally, he was prone to verbal outbursts, including hurling profanity at other members of the unit. On more than one occasion, Matt engaged in physical altercations with sailors who irked him in one way or another. If you wrote a book about how to be a shitty military member, Matt would be the protagonist.

Why the hell did the US Navy allow a turd like that to get away with his attitude and not kick him out? Because when you are in a war, you don't fire anyone. We were operational and in the combat zone, and to get rid of a certified technician, even if he was an absolute ass, was unpalatable for leadership. They feebly tried to hold Matt accountable for his actions and attitude, but he always found an excuse or a reason things didn't get done. Leaders rolled their eyes, turned away, and disengaged whenever an issue with Matt came up. His attitude and execution were cancerous and eventually resulted in a real risk to our team.

VBSS boardings never happen at 3:00 p.m.; it's always a 0-dark-30 thing. I had just finished a 10-hour work-and-watch rotation, showered, and gotten into my rack (a Navy bed about the size of a coffin and not quite as comfortable) when the call came over the loudspeaker: "Now set VBSS phase 2." That meant roll out of your rack, run to the armory, grab your gear, and head to the small boat to begin a launch.

Almost immediately, the other nine members of the VBSS team, our boat operator, and I were on the deck, ready to go. In less than 20 minutes, we were in the water and on our way to intercept an Iraqi tanker illegally moving oil into Iranian waters. Our intercept course put us squarely between Iraqi Navy ships and Iranian waters patrolled and defended by Iranian Navy small boats, which were of course not thrilled with our presence in the area. As we were moving expeditiously to the intercept point, the engine of the boat we were piloting stopped. It did not sputter and die, and it did not chug out. It just stopped working, dead as a doornail. Typically, when that type of thing happened, one of the crew attempted a fix; but when we opened the engine compartment, acrid black smoke billowed out. The engine had eaten itself due to a lack of oil pressure and a cascading failure. "Shit" was the only word that any of us could muster. Now we were faced with a real calamity.

Our team was stuck in a useless boat in the middle of hostile territory, blacked out (no lights on), and drifting directly into Iranian waters. Our communications worked, and we were in contact with the Cape St. George, but we were roughly seven miles away. One choice was to hold out and float along, praying we would somehow avoid drifting into Iranian coastal waters or be run over by the very tanker we were sent to intercept. Or we could radio the ship and request a pickup, which meant the cruiser would have to break off its air defense of the aircraft carrier to rescue us. Needless to say, the radio calls were unpleasant.

"USS Cape St. George, this is VBSS-1. We have had an engine failure and need an immediate pickup," our senior enlisted leader said into the radio.

"VBSS-1, this is CG-71. Is there no one onboard who can repair the boat and get the team back?" came the response from the ship.

"Well, there is no engine anymore. So I don't think so. We need pickup as we are adrift in the shipping channel and are at risk of a collision with traffic."

It got much more combative after that between our senior enlisted and the ship leadership, but the long and short of it was that Cape St. George had to break off air cover to come pick us up. It was another nine hours before we were rescued. Once we were back aboard the ship, the scale of the screw-up that resulted from Matt's and our leadership's failures got the Admiral for the Battle Group involved. Nothing motivates a leadership fix in the military like people with stars on their shoulders asking, "Why did this happen?"

A Navy cruiser is not a fuel-efficient vessel, and moving that beast at high speed to pick up a boat full of drifters required all engines at full bore. The toleration of Matt's failures, attitude, and abdication of duty, combined with our leadership's continual acceptance of a sailor's manipulation of the system, resulted in hundreds of thousands of dollars spent on fuel and a significant allocation of personnel to recover us. The Iraqi vessel managed to slide by during this fiasco, and the small boat was an absolute loss. One sailor's attitude and dereliction of duty affected an entire battle group.

While this story sounds like something that could only happen in the military, it is an all-too-common scenario in business as well. Have you ever had someone in or around your team who was a bad apple, whose attitude and actions were so caustic and corrosive that each time they entered the room, the air was sucked out of it? I would bet you have. How often did that person affect the group's—or, in some cases, the business's—ability to get things done? I would also bet that those people stayed around far too long, and you wondered why leadership didn't get rid of them. In almost every business I have met or consulted with, I have observed these types of people. Everyone knows they are bad for business and detrimental to the team's effectiveness.

Leadership knows those people need to go. They do. But usually, leadership doesn't want to deal with the fallout of a person being fired or asked to leave: the paperwork and the potential legal issues that follow. Just like the military, your organization is at war and needs to focus on its mission. Your business is always looking to sharpen its competitive edge, and it's easier and less disruptive to tolerate a bad apple than it is to do what you must and move that person on to greener pastures. But you will never *not* be at war. As long as you are in business, there will never be a good time to fire or transition someone. Just as in my Navy scenario, because of the logistical requirements and operational needs of the environment, there is never a point when all is well and uncomfortable actions become comfortable.

This can and does happen in the executive suite, too. Executives are not immune from being that person who needs to go.

Case in point: Shortly after my medical retirement from the US Navy, I went to work in the private sector for a globally known company that was a leader in its space. At the top of the food chain in the organization was an older gentleman I will call Rob. Rob was lauded by the company and in some industry circles as an innovator and thought leader. The first time I met the man, he seemed nice but slightly odd and disheveled. I could tell from the clothes he wore that he had money, and his constant bragging about his stable of race cars and performance machines made it clear that he had come into a substantial amount of cash at some point in his career. But that's not uncommon, so I thought, "Sure, he must know something to be this respected."

As our time together progressed, however, Rob was never on time. He was never dressed appropriately for any occasion; he often looked like his kids had dressed him. He was constantly the single point of focus in business meetings because he was the person customers wanted to talk to, but he was never there. Rob was always off on some mission doing clandestine things for the US government. Somehow, Rob managed to get himself tangentially brought into projects that he could never tell the team about and that magically precluded him from ever participating in any regular work or meetings. He was at best a ghost who lumbered into meetings late and without any knowledge of what the hell we were all doing.

But the C Suite and other executives raved about Rob's leadership and past innovations. He was an industry icon, and because of his achievements, we should all "put up with his idiosyncrasies." However, that could only go so far. We were trying to build a startup within the larger organization, and we honestly needed Rob to be deeply engaged in that effort and bring whatever magic he had to the team. If he was such an awesome innovator and leader, we needed him to participate with us—but that never happened. As a matter of fact, Rob was so out of it and removed from participation and collaboration that the group's leadership, the CEO of the bigger company, had to hire a handler for him. That person, who was eminently overqualified for this glorified babysitter role, was tasked with making sure Rob was on time and mentally present for meetings and events.

His handler was also to ensure that Rob dressed appropriately and was pleasant with customers, analysts, team members, and other leaders. It was disturbing to watch a grown man being babied by an extremely qualified person just to keep him from screwing up constantly. It was so bad that on more than one occasion, Rob forgot dress shirts and ties for his suits. This meant his handler not only had to buy him shirts but also had to iron them, as Rob would simply pull them out of the package and shuffle off to whatever he was involved in. His handler also had to tie his ties and visually inspect Rob before he met with anyone.

People noticed. Everyone either made jokes about the situation and tried to be accepting or shrugged their shoulders and did their best to pick up the slack caused by Rob's constant disruption. I could not figure out why Rob was so respected—but after doing some digging, I learned that most of his "achievements" were a combination of coming from money and being in the right industry at the right time. Rob had money. Boatloads of it. But it didn't come from him building any specific technology or business operation. He had simply ridden the wave of technology across various industries and been lucky enough to goof his way into acquisitions that had compounded. The only credit

I will give him as a leader is that Rob concealed his lack of talent and somehow made himself into a respected persona. It was all a veil, though; Rob made his money legally, but he did not deserve the acclaim and respect he was provided. Rob had no mental or physical handicaps; he was a slob and a lazy worker.

Over time, Rob's continued issues caused the collapse of our entire business unit. No successes and not a single customer came from his leadership or connections. Not customers ever signed up for the service, either. That lack of customer acquisition might not have been entirely Rob's fault, but he repeatedly missed meetings, and his attitude on customer calls was abrasive. Rob sure as hell didn't help us acquire any customers. He did nothing for the group or the company but rack up expensive dinners with clients "only he could meet with." His constant bumbling, tardiness, brash attitude, and lack of professionalism alienated important industry relations. His only real contribution was being such a thorn in everyone's side that each team member left as soon as they figured out the man in charge was basically an overpaid teenager. In less than 16 months, the business unit imploded and all the team members left. The company missed out on a growing segment of the market because of one person: Rob.

Rob might have been valuable to the group if he had been paraded around as a figurehead, because that's what he was. His value was in the persona he had built, and, in total honesty, he made some connections that might have turned into business. But as the saying goes, "The juice wasn't worth the squeeze." Rob was detrimental to operational needs, and his added tax on the group was a weight that dragged us all down. Watching management tolerate Rob and seeing our leadership encourage his continued problems by hiring someone to handle him only added to the issues. He needed to go; everyone knew it. But no one in a position of power was willing to make that call. Our team could only put up with the Rob game for so long. And like anywhere else in life, when things get too troubling for the group, the group either moves on or breaks up.

So, what should you get out of these experiences as a leader? Simply put, you get what you expect and deserve what you tolerate. That's it. If you lead your organization by allowing laziness and enabling unprofessional behavior, you deserve what happens. And you will get just that: laziness and unprofessionalism. It's a binary equation. Crap in equals crap out. Does that mean you must emulate Patton's brash and derisive leadership style, berating or physically abusing your employees? No. But you must be quick to address noted behaviors and actions that are outside the bounds of what you want for your team. Whatever you tolerate is what you will get. It's not only a business phenomenon but also a fact of how humans operate. It's more comfortable to just exist, be lazy, and barely scrape by. And for many, barely scraping by works just fine. They are operating in sanctioned work roles and know they are unlikely to be fired in today's world for various reasons.

Tolerating diva behavior from an executive is just as bad as, or worse than, accepting subpar behavior from others in the group. Grown people expect to be treated like adults, and they expect their leadership to act as such. Having a person in a C-level role be handled and managed like a runaway toddler will only lead to a lack of respect for your entire team over time. It becomes taxing and makes the person who is being handled a priority over everyone else's needs and the needs of the business. Even if that senior person is the all-time business winner of the universe, having them on the team and integrated into everyday operations is a bad idea. If you must retain that person on as a show pony, keep them in the barn: fed, rested, and quiet until it's time to trot them out.

As the leader, you are responsible for the team's outcomes. Period. Good, bad, ugly, whatever; it's up to you. Your team's perception of you as their leader hangs on whether you allow and enable any individual who runs rogue. If you tolerate small instances of disrespect and lack of discipline, very quickly you will allow larger and more frequent failures. The snowball of misery is formed on the mountain of bad behavior and unprofessionalism. Once it starts rolling downhill, nothing can stop it. Don't allow that to happen. Address what needs to be dealt with quickly, professionally, and often. Don't be afraid to remove a bad employee and have the intestinal fortitude to walk them out the door if you must. Your team will know what you expect and understand what they need to do not to be that bad actor.

4

Flat Organization, Flat Fail

We began to realize that by building a company with a flat org structure, we had done the exact opposite of what we had intended.

—Chris Savage, CEO, Wistia

Since the late 2000s, the idea of a flat organizational structure has become an industry norm, especially in the tech space. As businesses like Zappos, Treehouse, Medium, GitHub, Buffer, and others took off, they championed a flat organizational structure with little hierarchy and few managerial layers. To the casual observer, this structure seems to make sense and even be a good thing. No bosses? Who doesn't like that? No real chain of command, and no one to report to? Also good. Less corporate politics with people screwing each other over to move up the ladder of success? Sign me up. A flat organization seems as close to how we all want to work as anyone could get. You do your job, everyone else does theirs, and all is well with the world. Except it doesn't work out that way.

You probably never heard or read that all the organizations that extolled the flat organization abandoned the concept. GitHub gave up on a flat organization as the company restructured in 2016 because of a need for organizational structure and hierarchy. Buffer moved away from the concept, and its CEO even penned a letter about it entitled "What We Got Wrong." Medium went back to a more formal organization because "Holacracy" (a term the company coined for a decentralized structure with teams working autonomously to achieve company goals) was getting in the way of getting things done. Treehouse returned to having managers and bosses when the board and CEO noted that not having defined leadership roles was naïve and counter to productivity. You get the point.

Those major companies, many of which were poster children for a flat organization, realized things weren't functioning and were driven to change their approach. The flat organizational structure works fine when your organization is extremely small, with fewer than a few dozen employees. But as the organization grows, this model is not sustainable. In other words, the bigger it gets, the harder it falls.

What those companies failed to address was the fact that the flat organizational model wasn't something they put in place strategically; rather, it was an adaptation of their early founding. When those companies launched, they were small enough to have one leader and everyone else on the same organizational plane; but as they achieved growth, the management requirements alone dictated that a hierarchical structure needed to be adopted. Because many people seek to avoid corporate politics and don't like the idea of a boss, the flat organizations attempted to ride out that model. Until they got bucked off, that is.

Medium noted that "the flat organizational model [made it] difficult to coordinate efforts at scale. In the purest expression of

Holacracy, every team has a goal and works autonomously to deliver the path to serve that goal. But for larger initiatives, which require coordination across functions, it is time-consuming and divisive to gain alignment." Not having managers and leaders with authority means the ability to coordinate and execute suffers. And the possibility of friction among equally empowered individuals is always present. Imagine a meeting where everyone is in charge and has equal authority. How does anything get done? It's unwise to engage in this model and hope the leaders rise and the others fall in line. People will simply spend their time trying to gain more authority in a system where there is no authority to be had. You need to choose your leaders and empower them to lead carefully. You must be sure that everyone who works with and for them understands who makes what calls and who has the final decision-making authority. If you don't, you are telling everyone that they're *all* decision-makers, which will harm the clarity and productivity of the organization.

Conceptually, a flat organization makes sense. Everyone is empowered, the best person to solve any specific problem steps up, and good things happen. But that's not how people work. Expecting people to step up when there is a possibility of failure, as there always is, ignores the human reality that no one wants to be responsible for that failure—especially in a corporate system where the success of initiatives, projects, and products leads to improved economic status. The Boston-based company Wistia found this very true as it grew from fewer than 5 to more than 70 employees. Wistia's CEO noted in a blog, "We began to realize that by engaging in a flat organizational structure, we were doing the exact opposite of what we wanted to do as a business. We had centralized the decision making, and were relying on a secret implicit structure to make progress happen. Every company has a structure. If you don't explicitly define your structure, then you are left with an implicit one, and that can stifle productivity. We had hoped that being flat would let us move faster and be more creative, but as we grew, we ended up with an unspoken hierarchy that slowed down our ability to execute." (Huczynski, Lack of clear structure and hierarchy: *The Pros and Cons of a Flat Organizational Structure*, 2013).

Jo Freeman, an American feminist, opined on this issue in an essay titled "The Tyranny of Structurelessness." It was based on her experience as part of a women's group in the 1960s that was an early adopter of the flat organizational model. She wrote elsewhere, "the apparent lack of structure too often disguised as informal, unacknowledged, and unaccountable leadership that was all the more pernicious because its very existence was denied" (O'Reilly, 2013). Jo meant that in the absence of a formal structure, one emerges. This happens for various reasons, but a significant one is that some people impose their will on others. Humans have done this since the dawn of time, and it should be expected in any organization. If we organically evolved structures for our groups in caves eons ago, why would we not do so now when we wear chinos and polo shirts instead of pelts to work? The organizational structure that forms when one has not been clearly delineated is chaos, and it's built on personality and informal communication channels. Employees who are not part of the clique that has installed this shadow leadership structure are outsiders, and they find it difficult to navigate the veiled structure.

Even Google, with all its prowess as a business, failed at the flat organizational approach. Larry Page noted in *Harvard Business Review* that when "we were about 400 people the flat organizational experiment fell apart after a few months. We tried to eliminate our managers as a position and what happened was everyone came to me for everything." Treehouse noted similar problems when it grew beyond 100 employees. The CEO lamented that projects didn't get done, and there was no one to hold accountable. A leader can only focus on so many things simultaneously, no matter how awesome they may be. Human beings can't operate at the scale of an entire company (Gotsis, 2020). Interestingly, employees at Google were thrilled when the manager position was returned, saying that they could now do just their job and not everyone else's. According to an article in the *Harvard Business Review*, Google is an engineering-led company; typically, engineers don't want to be micromanaged at the project level but are more than happy to be managed at the career level. Having managers in the organization meant engineers could build things and not worry about travel reports and bureaucracy.

Let me provide an example from my experience working in a flat organization. For this one, I will call the leader Dave. Dave had been the CEO of two startups, both of which had been acquired, and he was proud of those achievements. Rightfully so, as any acquisition is a feather in one's cap. However, Dave cut his teeth working in large organizations as a head of sales and essentially wound up CEO for the two startups because he could sell ice cubes to penguins and was good at meeting his numbers. Dave had also seen how slow and bureaucratic the big companies were, and when he got free from them, he focused on building lean teams and small organizations designed around a flat structure. So, Dave believed his two startup successes were thanks to his leadership in a flat organization. Both startups were acquired in less than two years and then reabsorbed into the Borg (larger companies).

Dave's current company employed roughly 100 people spread across the globe, with the largest group of 40 employees hammering out code for the company's product in a development shop overseas. Elsewhere, Dave had assembled small, nimble sales teams of fewer than five people in different regions, and the other departments consisted of no more than seven personnel. Dave constantly trumpeted about the flat organization and how everyone was empowered to do their job. He claimed all his subordinate leaders had full authority to enact change and execute. But nothing could be further from the truth.

With no formal structure and the reality that Dave brought his past startup team—all alphas—into this new business, he had essentially created competing fiefdoms. No subordinate leader had the authority to do anything, including in the large offshore development shop. Whenever one business unit leader attempted to execute an action they thought was good for the business, the other unit leaders immediately ran to Dave for follow-ups. The kingdom of developers was in the power position and was the only group able to flat-out ignore and deny other valid business requests made to the team. They were building the product that made the money, and therefore, they should be able to do what they wanted. So at every turn, the development team's leader contacted Dave to help them with their goals and tasking while ignoring or torpedoing other initiatives. Telling the leadership team to "run their route" didn't help because both the offense and defense got their direction from Dave.

No one had a clear line of communication or authority other than to "talk to Dave." He was the company's CEO and the choke point of any progress or success. The warring fiefdoms played a constant game of "If mommy says no, go ask daddy," and the company's success stagnated.

Dave was the single point of authority, and one person could not handle managing the many moving parts of a globally distributed organization. Nor can one person maneuver through a global business's cultural and societal differences. So, Dave was constantly physically and mentally taxed to the max. Frustration, anger, and simmering resentment grew among the employees. Meetings were always contentious; screaming matches ensued, with occasional threats of physical violence during meetings of executives and team members. On a good day, no one talked, and some things got done. On a bad day, the business resembled a kindergarten filled with angry toddlers who needed a nap encircling a ragged teacher who could only cry as she looked on in horror at the never-ending tussle. But Dave wanted a flat organization, and he certainly got one. One that flat failed.

The simplest way to summarize this story is to reiterate what I said initially: you get what you deserve, and you deserve what you tolerate. I bet most leaders have a very good understanding of what is taking place—at least, they should—and they know the powerful personalities in their organization. Without structure and clear lines of authority and communication, stronger-willed employees impose their will on weaker personalities, and a de facto structure and hierarchy will emerge. Tolerating this and the resulting insufficient performance, disrespect, and any other less-than-optimal attitudes will lead to chaos and significantly impact employee morale and operational success. Major organizations were smart enough to realize that a flat organizational model was doomed to fail, and they quickly pivoted away from that experiment. Being flat works if your organization is small. As soon as you have double-digit numbers of employees, it's time to change.

Set your organization up for success and empower your trusted employees to "run their route." If you ignore the need for structure and remove the human desire for leadership and accountability, you will get exactly what you deserve: chaos, failed projects, and a never-ending lack of communication.

CHAPTER

5

Don't Be a Dumpster Chicken

Seagull managers fly in, make a lot of noise, dump on everyone, then fly out.

—Ken Blanchard

Have you ever been near the ocean and heard the distant caw of a seagull? I remember vividly being in the Navy and hearing and seeing seagulls surrounding the dumpsters at the end of the pier. I also remember seeing seagulls fighting and screeching at one another as they clashed over any scrap of food they could find. Seagulls are the instigators of the marine avian world. A seagull will see other birds sitting around waiting for a meal, swoop in, make a lot of noise, crap on whatever is in range, and fly away. A dominant seagull will also squawk at larger animals to make their presence known and let that bigger animal know they are unhappy with its presence. Seagulls fight, caw, shit on, and impose their will on whatever they can at every opportunity, even if there is no reason or merit to their argument.

Seagulls are so motivated to swoop down and impose on other animals that they have been noted "attacking sharks near the surface of the water." As you can imagine, more than a few unlucky or nearsighted seagulls have found themselves the victims of that tactic. When one desires to actively engage in the wrong space, one often messes with the wrong perceived victim. In the marine world, that means one ends up as shark shit.

In the Navy, we called seagulls "dumpster chickens." I don't recall hearing any particularly useful or factual discussion about why that moniker fell on seagulls, but it stuck. Ask any sailor what a "dumpster chicken" is, and they will point to the nearest seagull with gusto. I would venture to say that the "chicken" part comes from seagulls being found in the middle of the ocean: if a sailor is afloat on a life raft, a seagull quickly becomes a chicken-ish dinner.

Being known as a DC (dumpster chicken) leader in the Navy is not a sign of respect, as you can probably imagine. Most often, DCs are junior officers, although, in some rarer instances, they are senior officers. However, the title of DC is very much earned; it is never given away. For a leader to be tagged as a DC, they must continually engage in what they consider leadership activities. I will provide some context for a DC I worked with while on active duty.

For this story, I will call the DC LT (lieutenant in Navy lingo). LT had been in the Navy for about seven years. He was a graduate of the US Naval Academy and, by all paperwork accounts, a stellar leader. Sure, that's what the paperwork said. But LT was the world's foremost DC. LT was tasked with being the officer in charge of my work center. He had an uncanny talent for never showing up for our morning daily meetings but miraculously appearing whenever something went awry. It was as if he had a radar for problems and could zero in on where and when something was off, even though there was no way he knew what was causing the issue.

The man could disappear for hours on a ship 567 feet long and no more than 55 feet wide. Somehow, he discovered a way to show up, say something (usually of little to no value, or in some cases, a straightforward revision of the chief's input), and then melt away amorphously into the ship's steel hull. Ninjas are less skilled at evading detection than this guy.

LT would, however, appear whenever something went wrong, as often happens out to sea, long enough to make his assessment. Then, he would magically depart with no one knowing why he had been there or what he planned to do to help with the situation. On many occasions, LT breezed by a problem area or meeting, loudly mumbled something as he strolled away, shuffling off to another "meeting." He always had a more important or pressing matter to attend to; even when the entire ship went dead in the water due to a massive engineering issue, LT was engaged elsewhere.

The only time LT engaged was when something happened that might affect how he was perceived among the other officers in the ship's wardroom. If a scenario of that heft was in play, LT was quickly on his way to squawk at maximum volume. When a career-impacting event occurred, LT swooped down from whatever event he had been engaged in (most likely a nap in his stateroom) and loudly and vociferously impose his thoughts about the needed solution for all to hear.

One such event is the Captain's Mast, which is like a military court martial. For a ship's officer, if one of their work center's sailors goes to the Captain's Mast, it is a career-impacting event. If a sailor finds themselves "standing tall at the mast," things have gone wrong. Horribly wrong. On such an occasion, one of LT's most junior sailors had been found asleep on watch. In wartime, sleeping on a watch is punishable by death.

Luckily for this junior sailor, we were not yet at war; this was in 1999 before the Global War on Terror began, but it was still a serious issue. LT was away working on other tasks when the work center Chief and leadership discussed the charges and offenses with the young sailor. But when the Captain's Mast went into full session, LT barged into the room like the feds raiding a meth lab.

LT was furious that one of his sailors had been found sleeping on watch and wanted this young sailor "kicked out of the Navy." LT stood directly in front of the accused sailor and interrupted the Captain as he made sure the accused understood his options. "Captain, Sir. Please get this turd out of my division and out of our Navy. Sir, he does not merit your time, and his conduct is corrosive to our work center." Bewildered, the Captain looked around, wondering why an LT was interrupting his Mast.

But before the Captain could unload what I can only assume would have been a tirade of epic proportions, the junior sailor asked the most pressing question.

"Who are you, lieutenant?" The young sailor said sheepishly.

LT looked around, baffled. How could this sailor not know that LT was his division officer? In what world could this squid not have known who his LT was? The rage boiled in LT with such force that it seemed he would burst out of his dress uniform. Like the mighty seagull he was, LT was seconds away from unleashing a squawk of epic proportions.

Being a 26-year Navy officer, the Captain, shook his head and calmly raised his hand. With the tone of a father asking his son a sincere question, the Captain said, "Shipmate, do you mean to tell me you don't know who your division officer is?" The Captain's words resounded throughout the room, echoing off the steel ceiling and parquet floor.

LT stopped mid-squawk and turned on his heel to face the Captain. Without a word, the Captain pointed to the nearest wall, indicating "go over there" to LT. LT took up position along the wall as if he were a kindergartener about to receive a lashing.

The Captain finished his Mast with the young sailor and punished him appropriately. The Captain's demeanor was calm but firm. The sailor and his leadership team, myself included, left the room as quickly as possible, following the Captain's directions to "get out." We all knew what was about to come.

Walking down the hall, we could hear the flurry of profanity aimed directly at LT. The Captain had discovered a seagull inside his ship and was not happy about it. The fact that LT tried to swoop in, act like Johnny Navy, and discuss terminating a sailor who did not even know LT existed was never going to sit well with the Captain. LT got the counseling session of his young career that day, and we never saw him again. The Captain ensured that the dumpster chicken could fly around some other dumpster on the waterfront and not shit further on the work center or affect his sailors.

Dumpster chickens aren't always leadership. As with the actual birds, you will often notice DCs flitting around others in different organizations, looking for an opportunity to dive in and caw about whatever problems might arise. It's just as critical that those DCs are kept away from imposing their will and thoughts on your employees who are doing their jobs. Keep an eye out for those seagulls that are circling constantly, and wave them off early and often. It's your responsibility as the person in charge to protect your workforce from dumpster chickens and keep them at bay at all costs.

Allow me to provide another example of a DC who was not in a leadership position but whose impact was still felt by the entire company. I will call this dumpster chicken PJ.

PJ came from the world of startups. He had spent his career helping companies get off the ground to build their products and roll their offerings out to their target market. PJ was great at writing code and building technology.

PJ had the chops to be a great head developer or designer. He possessed a unique ability to be both a coder and a product visionary who saw the niche in the market that his technology could fill. But PJ also said, "I do what I want when I want to." He should never have been in a leadership position. Ever.

In my interactions with him, PJ never did much more than shit on others' ideas and find ways to bring them down. He was adept at being the high-flying dumpster chicken that constantly cawed at others while he circled just out of their reach. He was not worried about contributing; he did this to get them to move away from his dumpster. PJ was ultra-territorial in his area of responsibility, and he did not play well with others. He appeared at leadership and organizational meetings when he "wasn't busy." Everyone knew there would be no successful outcome anytime PJ attended a meeting. The team would listen to his squawking about what would and wouldn't work based on his experience and the requirements of his code and technology.

Meetings with PJ involved dissolved into finger-pointing and bickering. Everyone in the room looked for someone else to blame for perceived or legitimate issues that PJ pointed out. However, even if the issue PJ discussed was real, he offered no solution. He only wanted to validate his brilliance by show-ing that he had found a problem with someone else's code or technology. PJ had no genuine desire to provide a fix. He was the ultimate DC, circling above the fray and squawking at those below him so he could bask in the chaos he created. The worst part was that when things got to a fever pitch, PJ would leave, quietly slinking out the nearest door or ending his Zoom link.

PJ also managed to maneuver his way into executive and boardroom-level conversations, where he played the same game. He was the best at "flying in and shitting" everywhere.

PJ was always late to board meetings, as he knew there would be fewer questions about why he was present when the meeting was already underway. He entered the room late, found a chair slightly outside the central seating positions, and waited for an opportune time to unleash his load of crap.

Whenever a conversation around a technical need or code issue arose, rather than offering solutions, PJ dive-bombed into the matter and introduced topics and problems that validated his exemplary knowledge. The board and the CEO would vector in on whatever issue PJ presented, as they relied on his "insights," but none of the leadership realized they were validating PJ's ego. They were not solving a problem. As usual, once the dumpster was covered in crap, PJ quietly flew away.

If you have seen the movie *Finding Nemo*, you probably remember a scene with Nemo and a group of seagulls intent on devouring the little fish. Each bird knows only one word: "Mine!" And they repeat that one word continuously throughout their scene with Nemo. Ultimately, the fish gets away, and the seagulls fly off into the blue sky after their failed attempts to eat him. Unlike the gulls in that scene, PJ didn't want ownership of things. It was never a focus for him to fix a problem, as that might reveal the terrible truth that he didn't have all the answers. It was best for PJ to point out problems, be loud about them, and act as if they mattered to him, but he did not own them. If PJ had been in the movie, his seagull character would have constantly been squawking, "Yours! Yours!"

This dumpster chicken behavior is much more common than most people realize or pay attention to. Most of the time, we hear DCs cawing from a distance, and we acknowledge that they are present, but we don't collectively realize how damaging they can be. The occasional swoop-in-and-crap seagull is one thing, but having one bird constantly dump on everyone is degrading to the organization. Seeing the executive team and board tolerate or encourage DC activities will also affect organizational morale and operational execution.

If you are in a leadership position and are aware of a DC circling overhead, find a way to either ward them off or clip their wings. Obviously, this doesn't mean you should do anything beyond the boundaries of smart HR practices. But you should aggressively limit that DC's ability to influence and impact your organization. You will often find that simply by making a DC's actions known to the group, the gull will realize everyone is aware of the behavior. DCs like to make noise but don't like to be a point of focus for long. Just as a seagull will swoop down, grab its target morsel, and flit away, a DC wants to slide in, grab the attention, and exit the interaction.

Many leaders will either tolerate a DC, which only empowers them, or in the most extreme cases, promote them. It's usually easier to silence the squawking than to deal with the problem. But problems that are not dealt with fester. Festering leads to rotting. Pay close attention to the seagulls circling your organization, and work to keep the "stink" down. After all, a smelly dumpster is often surrounded by dumpster chickens, and that's the last problem anyone wants.

CHAPTER

6

Go Slow to Be Fast

Slow is Smooth, and Smooth is Fast

—U.S. Navy SEALs

In most businesses and in life, the goal is often to go as fast as possible. This is especially applicable in technology. Every technology leader you encounter is working to be first to market. Silicon Valley is teeming with technology companies and start-ups focused on fast execution and growth at all costs. Entire development methodologies, such as agile development, are built around this concept. Do what you can with what you have, make it work, iterate, and push forward. Always forward. Faster than the competition means victory. At least, that is the thinking.

Look at the world of application (app) development. Before 2020, the average time to develop an app and get it to market was around 12 months from start to finish (Julia Basysta, How to correctly estimate your app development timeline, 2020). For a more extended app development project, the timeline before 2020 could be as long as 18 months, including the time for market research and product validation. In 2023, an app can be produced fully, including market research and product validation, in a rough average of fewer than nine months.

Although improving development speed by three months may not seem like much, that development speed today means that in March 2023, approximately 31,500 mobile apps were released through the Apple App Store (Statista, 2023). That number was up by 2 percent compared to the previous month. In the Android world, the numbers are even more staggering. In February 2023, approximately 87,000 mobile apps were released through the Google Play Store—more than twice the number of IOS applications (Statista, 2023),

I remember hearing a story on this topic from a Marine friend who had been on patrol in Helmand Province, Afghanistan. He had unknowingly led his team into a minefield (near dusk, no less). One might ask, "How does this happen?" In a combat environment, it is easy to stumble into a trap, such as a minefield. It takes seconds and one wrong decision or navigation error to accidentally stroll onto death's doorstep. The choices my Marine friend faced were potentially life-threatening, and his immediate reaction was to find a way out "as fast as fucking possible." But moving quickly while not knowing where to step would lead to death or dismemberment, and probably both.

Additionally, he needed to keep track of each step he took while leading his team. At the time, they were focused on a mission objective, not walking, and that needed to change. As he stood still as a statue, his pulse raced. His eyes were wide. His team members all stood motionless, looking at each other, fear strewn across their faces. He told me his heart was beating so hard that the buttons on his fatigues were visibly bouncing. The enemy was out there somewhere. In less than an hour, the Marine fire team needed to extricate themselves from standing in a killing field.

So, what could he do? How could he get himself and his team out of the ring of death? He slowed down. He explained the scenario to me as follows.

First, the Marine had to make a critical decision about whether to break radio silence and inform his superior, or just move. Breaking radio silence might have revealed his location to the enemy, which is never a good thing when you are on patrol, especially when you and your entire fire team are standing inside the kill zone of a minefield. His other option was to make the risky decision to press on. Choosing the first option, he nervously waited for the response from his commander, which came quickly in a calm and assured tone. "Take your time, sort yourself out, think, and be calm. Let me know when you are back on track." The Marine later described that short but intensely focused advice from his superior as the best example of leadership he had experienced in his 32-year career.

Still standing in the minefield, the Marine looked at his team and took the initiative. He calmly and slowly motioned for each team member to do as he did, one by one. He was the first to calmly, slowly, turn on his heel and begin the careful transition to safety.

The Marine commanded his team members to move into a line directly behind him as he studied the dirt at his feet. With each step, he cautiously looked for footprints his or his team had made, indicating that someone had already safely stepped in a particular spot. Slowly, carefully, and quietly, they extricated themselves from the minefield.

The Marine and his team marked the location for demolition, maneuvered far around the killing field, and continued their mission. He told me it probably took only a few minutes, but each step felt like hours. Time slowed, and all that mattered was their vision and focus on the minute details in the dirt that would keep them alive. The team was saved through a combination of focus, careful movement, teamwork, and smooth speed of action.

The Marine team in a minefield is a stellar example of a place and time when moving fast is impossible—moving any faster than one careful step at a time meant at least severe injury and, more than likely, death. Standing still was not an option, either. Each second they delayed making decisions and acting meant the enemy had additional time to vector in on them. Additionally, if a Marine were either injured or killed, their fellow Marines would do their best to come to their aid, leading to more catastrophe. Marines do not leave fallen behind, ever. The only solution was to practice the mantra of "slow is smooth, and smooth is fast."

In business, although we will never face the absolute calamity a literal minefield presents, there are times when we may find ourselves standing still, facing inevitable failures. Every fiber of our being will drive us to "move" and to "get the fuck out of there" as fast as we can. However, hasty action in most scenarios will also increase the likelihood of failure. As we lead our teams out of the failure zone, we must maintain our focus, move cautiously, and avoid panic and knee-jerk reactions.

As leaders, we must also remind ourselves that it is our job to keep the focus on what matters most and, when things get "fast," remind our team to slow down.

Let me detail a business scenario I was part of where going fast seemed like a great idea—even a need—but speed was the enemy of success. Ultimately, fast execution in this endeavor cost the company significantly.

After my stint at a research organization, I was offered a position as an executive with a small company. This business had been operating for over 24 years and languished at roughly the same revenue and growth rate. The company's leadership sought to modify and adapt the company's legacy digital communication technology for cybersecurity-specific use cases. This made sense, as the legacy solution was aligned to offering a needed security capability, and at the time, the market was ripe for additional growth in this vertical.

Our team set out to reinvent this two-decade-old company and revamp the legacy technology into a security offering. It made sense both logically and organizationally to modify the legacy connection solution into one focused on enabling secure connectivity and protected web access.

The market opportunity, however, like all opportunities, was fleeting. The security market was becoming inundated with solutions that all offered similar capabilities. If we were to have a share of the market, we needed to move quickly. At least, that was the mandate from the board and the CEO.

"Go, run your route. Sell. Get clients and partners." That was the weekly mantra from the CEO as we tried to run parallel threads for the company's growth. On the one hand, we had developers coding up the solution to try to beat the competition in the market. On the other hand, our sales and partner leaders were actively selling and working to grow our channel offering.

But we were doing this so quickly that the sales agreements and partner needs outpaced the development efforts. We did not even have a viable product to sell. We had a cobbled-together, glorified demonstration instance that we convinced ourselves was good enough to show-and-tell with our customers and partners. While the fake-it-until-you-make-it approach is common in technology, selling before you have a product is also a widespread practice; we were moving too fast and gambling that we would deliver value before we had value to offer.

The CEO made promises to the board and the company founders, setting highly ambitious sales goals based on this new product offering—the one that didn't exist. This only threw gas on the fire and forced us to press forward at a breakneck speed. In less than a quarter, the company lined up many customers; but when those customers started asking for product delivery, they got a barely functional and often buggy solution. Had any of those customers researched the product they received, they would have quickly realized this was a digital shell game of the highest order.

The speed of the sales outpaced the ability to deliver the product. Customers and partners were signed up and onboarded, but the technology needed to live up to the hype, and it couldn't.

The whole business was a cat-herding fiasco. Our support team and developers constantly handled customer outages, feature requests, and stability issues—all bad things for a security solution that is supposed to be always on and consistently securing the user. Additionally, it did not take long for the more experienced partners to realize they had been flimflammed and given a marginally valuable product. This allowed the partners to revise their contracts and threaten to take their business elsewhere. All because we focused on speed to market and the opportunity, not actual customer needs.

The insanity and sales shenanigans ultimately caused the company to "take a step back." That meant we lost a quarter of our business opportunities, as we had to take the product into a holding stage and focus on the technology. For three months, we watched the market develop, solidify, and roll right by us as we fumbled to get the solution to the level our customers deserved. Of course, the entire time we were in limbo, getting things fixed as they should have been from the start, the CEO and board were still pushing and scrambling for sales. Things were not in a good place.

As the CSO, I accept full responsibility for this failure. My job was to be sure we followed a strategic, thoughtful approach to this rollout. I was tasked with ensuring that we would launch this capability into the market correctly and achieve our metrics as we followed a well-planned path to execution. None of that happened. I should have been louder during our meetings. I failed our team by letting the CEO and board manipulate our proposed strategy to get into the market smartly. They wanted immediate sales and growth and were hell-bent on "not letting the market pass us by." This was one of the best learning environments I ever participated in. I watched as the drive to numbers and metrics gutted my strategy, and I observed how speed to market engendered failure.

The company should have met its goals for the year but did not because of the ineffective approach to the market opportunity.

You cannot lose an entire quarter of business, have partners strong-arm you to adjust contracts, roll back a technology offering, and meet "stretch sales goals." Ultimately, the company climbed back out of that pit of despair. But while the company managed to get back into solid growth numbers, it did so only to meet the most significant economic downturn in 50 years. The opportunity and market dynamics changed almost overnight. The exit was an abysmal failure in monetary terms. A financial windfall was washed away by the deluge that combined a lousy economy, lost time for execution, and a shoddy early market approach. The only people significantly rewarded financially were those who had been at the company the longest, who honestly deserved it most—and, of course, the board and CEO.

7

Beware the Brilliant Jerk. . .

Don't be a jerk. Even if you are brilliant, don't be a brilliant jerk.
—Girish Mathrubhootam

We must deal with a brilliant jerk at work at some point in our careers. Brilliant jerks are everywhere; sometimes, they are even CEOs. Other times, the brilliant jerk is the head of technology, or they might be a customer service person. But they exist. Unfortunately, in most organizations, the brilliant jerk gets praised by management while making everyone else's life a living hell. Sometimes, their jerkiness is recognized—confusingly, their attitude may be foolishly endorsed or accepted as quirkiness. Other times, their toxicity goes unnoticed by the people in the executive suite, but the impact of these corrosive personalities is never unknown to those who work with them directly.

Everyone can be a jerk. I am a jerk monthly for a variety of reasons. I also freely admit that if you asked 100 people about me, a few of them would certainly say, "That guy is a jerk." That's fine; everyone has their bad days. What we are talking about here is the employee who is continually a jerk. Most often, this jerkiness comes from an amalgamation of ego and a lack of solid interpersonal skills. I have often seen the brilliant jerk openly deriding others within an organization. Brilliant jerks are typically okay with pointing out other people's failures and shortcomings as they sit on their throne of jerkdom. However, if anyone challenges the jerk, the jerk ups their corrosive attitude. When the jerk is held to account, their fragile ego crumbles as they cannot stand to be called to the carpet, even when a problem arises directly from the jerk's actions.

A great example of a corporation that has embraced the no-brilliant-jerk mantra is Netflix. Since the start of the pandemic, Netflix has benefited substantially. The company's stock price has increased by roughly 40 percent since 2020, to the mid-$550s, and as of 2023, its market cap exceeded $240 billion. That number exceeded that of The Walt Disney Company, which has far more in the way of tangible assets and intellectual property and is an American corporate icon. Netflix's membership in its global streaming service has also increased dramatically. The company now has 193 million subscribers in 190 countries.

Netflix has done all this while having a company policy of no brilliant jerks. While not all of Netflix's success can be attributed to that one no-brilliant-jerks rule, the fact that the company has made it a policy to avoid jerks is notable. In the simplest terms, Netflix has done well for various reasons, but not having to deal with the turnover and other HR issues caused by brilliant jerks certainly helps.

According to the book *The No Asshole Rule* by Robert I. Sutton, Ph.D., we can use a test to determine whether a potential employee might be an asshole or a jerk. Simply put, the test consists of these two questions:

- After encountering the person, do people feel oppressed, humiliated, or otherwise worse about themselves?
- Does the person target people who are less powerful than they are?

That seems simple. I can immediately think of a bevy of people I have known personally and professionally for whom the answers to those questions would be a resounding "Yup." Research also notes that brilliant jerks have a somewhat standard set of readily identifiable behaviors (Heskett, 2014). Among those behaviors are the following:

- They're prone to unpredictable outbursts and are verbally abusive.
- They're extraordinarily talented and intelligent, charismatic, and persuasive, but they're never pleased with results, driven to gain personal recognition, and blind to the costs of their behavior.
- They cause workplace friction and conflict, spread rumors, and sabotage others.
- They engage in psychological bullying and can even be physically threatening.
- They show callousness and a lack of empathy.
- They have a grandiose sense of self-worth.
- They fail to accept responsibility for their actions and always look to place blame elsewhere.

Most of us have had to work for someone like that at some point in our careers. Sadly, besides changing jobs ourselves, the only hope we usually have is that the brilliant jerk changes jobs or quits. Most brilliant jerks have a high IQ; they are technically smart but also have a low EQ (emotional intelligence). Brilliant jerks have quick analytical minds and expertise that can help turn around ailing departments, companies, hospitals, or non-profits. That is their value; they can bring solutions to bear faster and typically more effectually than others. But what is that value worth to your organization? Are you willing to gamble your growth and future on a single person being the point of potential failure? There are very few Steve-Jobs-level brilliant jerks out there. What is the likelihood that you have employed the next one?

Brilliant jerks bring monetary value to an organization and have been the leaders of companies and organizations. Most brilliant jerks' value is almost entirely limited to the business's financial side, and even that can be fleeting. A brilliant jerk will continually degrade your business culture, ultimately affecting the bottom line. Culture and the absence of people who negatively impact that business culture are so influential that according to research from FTSE Russell, companies on the Fortune 100 Best Companies to Work For® list outperform the market by a factor of 3.36. Three percent may not seem like much, but consider that amount compounding over time (Kitterman, 2023). In a 10-year time frame, that's over 30 percent growth just by not having negative people around. Additionally, companies that avoid allowing a brilliant jerk to impact their culture negatively see better than a 50 percent reduction in turnover (Kitterman, 2023). Given that, on average, a new hire costs a company roughly $5,000 that turnover cost adds up quickly. Brilliant jerks hinder productivity and can derail progress, which is bad for business.

Even the President of the United States has had problems with brilliant jerks. In 2021, President Biden appointed his then-science advisor to be the head of the Office of Science and Technology Policy (OSTP), a cabinet-level role in the administration. Dr. Eric Lander is a distinguished biologist and geneticist, and the role he took is the highest scientific office in the

U.S. government. The scientific community lauded this appointment as a clear sign that science now sat at the right hand of the most powerful office in the land. After the COVID issues of 2020–2023, having a senior scientist appointed to this office was noted as nothing short of earth-shattering in the scientific community.

However, that welcome news was short-lived. The awe was replaced by shock and sadness as Lander, one of science's most celebrated stars, resigned less than three months after his appointment. His resignation followed allegations of abusive behavior toward subordinates, particularly women. Rachel Wallace, who served as general counsel at OSTP under Lander, filed a formal complaint for conduct she described as "egregious." Furthermore, Ms. Wallace noted that "many professional women have been left in tears, traumatized, and feeling vulnerable and isolated."

A subsequent investigation found evidence of "bullying" by Lander. There was also "credible evidence of instances of multiple women having complained to other staff about negative interactions with Dr. Lander." In his resignation letter, Dr. Lander wrote,

> I am devastated that I caused hurt to past and present colleagues by how I have spoken to them. I have sought to push myself and my colleagues to reach our shared goals—including, at times, challenging and criticizing. But it is clear that things I said, and the way I said them, crossed the line at times into being disrespectful and demeaning to both men and women.

But it was not just one or two people who noted this disrespectful and toxic behavior by the brilliant jerk who was in charge. Out of an office of 140 people, 14 reported they had similar experiences with Dr. Lander. That means 1 in 10 people had significantly negative interactions with a leader appointed by the most powerful office in the United States. And this went on for months. Nine of 14 other witnesses and former OSTP staffers said Lander yelled and humiliated people in front of their peers. This behavior contradicts the boss's (the president's) policy that "anyone who disrespected their colleagues would be fired on the spot. No ifs, ands, or buts."

Ms. Wallace, a career civil servant across the executive branch since the Clinton administration, had seen more than her fair share of gruff and abrasive behavior. But Dr. Lander took the cake. During her deposition, she noted that Lander "retaliated against staff for speaking out and asking questions by calling them names, disparaging them, embarrassing them in front of their peers, laughing at them, shunning them, taking away their duties, and replacing them or driving them out of the agency." All those actions and behaviors are associated with the brilliant-jerk problem.

After the investigation, the White House's personnel and counsel's offices concluded that Lander's offenses were "very, very serious and are outside the expectations of all staff within the [Executive Office of the President]." They also concluded that he had violated the White House's Safe and Respectful Workplace Policy. But what was done about the issues that the White House faced because of Dr. Lander? Was he fired as required by the policy that President Biden had described publicly? No. Instead of being disciplined, Lander was expected to hold even more meetings with subordinates. The White House also mandated training on the workplace policy for all staff. In this case, the supremely responsible party, the president, chose to make the many suffer for the sins of the few. Even though one person was directly responsible for the problems and was clearly outside the bounds of an established practice, no real punishment was awarded.

On the contrary, everyone was punished by having to do additional training and continue to meet with someone they all knew was a jackass.

During his inauguration, President Biden stated, "If you are ever working with me and I hear you treat another colleague with disrespect, talk down to someone, I promise you I will fire you on the spot. On the spot. No ifs, ands, or buts." But that didn't happen in this case. And if you recall from the earlier chapter on how you deserve what you tolerate, the only responsible party here is the president for not holding Dr. Lander to account. The effects of this failure are already showing up in the OSTP staff. Some OSTP staffers now scoff at the president's promise as empty political rhetoric.

Dr. Eric Lander clearly earns the description "brilliant," too. He is a stellar scientist and a valuable member of the scientific community. He won a MacArthur Foundation Genius award in 1987 at age 30 and worked on the international Human Genome Project and CRISPR-based genome editing. He was one of the nation's leading scientists for decades and was instrumental in developing the COVID vaccine. However, Lander had a long history as a brash, polarizing figure. He had all the hallmarks of a brilliant jerk, yet he was put in a leadership position, and that decision led to additional drama for the president's team to deal with.

Ultimately, having Lander resign meant that the position had to be restaffed, and the office of the president had to deal with the perception that they appointed a jerk to an extremely high position. The benefit that the brilliant jerk brought to the office was negated by his demeanor and the negativity that followed him. The investigation, additional training, impact on culture, and added hiring process of a subsequent employee wasted time and resources for the highest office in the land.

Be exceptionally cautious about who you hire for any leadership role. A brilliant person might be valuable and could help the bottom line, but is their impact on your culture and employees worth it? Do you have the time and bandwidth to deal with the issues a toxic person might bring? If the answer to either of those questions is a "maybe not," then avoid that hire.

8

Money, the Root of All Evil (But It May Yield the Fruit of Success)

I love money. I love everything about it. I bought some pretty good stuff. Got me a $300 pair of socks. Got a fur sink. An electric dog polisher. A gasoline powered turtleneck sweater. And, of course, I bought some dumb stuff, too.

—Steve Martin, *The Jerk*

In the comedy classic *The Jerk*, Steve Martin plays a jerk; well, a raging idiot is more accurate. Anyway, he does this exceptionally well. One of the funniest things that his character, Navin R. Johnson, does is stumble accidentally upon an innovative way of keeping a customer's glasses from sliding off their nose. The customer tells Navin, a gas station attendant, "The damn things keep falling." Navin, who lives to please others, immediately jumps into the gas station garage and affixes a bridge to the client's glasses that will keep the glasses in place on his nose. The client tries them on and is so impressed with them that he tells Navin, "I know people who invest in this type of stuff." Fast-forward a bit in the movie, and Navin has a giant house, a beautiful wife, nice socks, and all kinds of useless, stupid crap. He is instantly rich because of the investors and the sales of his little eyeglasses stabilizer. The problem is that the small bridge in the center of the glasses causes the wearer's eyes to drift to the center and focus on the glasses stabilizer, and millions of people become cross-eyed as a result.

It's a great movie, and if you haven't seen it and you enjoy a good comedy, watch it. It's hilarious, but *The Jerk* is also a cautionary tale. Although few Silicon Valley tech entrepreneurs are as clueless as Navin Johnson, many stumble into the money-chasing rat race. Often, those technology wizards have created a great piece of technology that genuinely solves a problem, much like Navin. Still, those innovators quickly focus only on the dollars and cents of running a business. And that shortsightedness, much like Navin's customers' crooked eyes, only distorts the reality that chasing the money puts the leaders and their employees on a hamster wheel they can't get off.

Let me summarize some of the more interesting points regarding funding in the technology and venture capital (VC) space. The first thing you should know is that although raising money seems exceptionally difficult, there is plenty of cash in and around technology, especially cybersecurity. There is always a VC investor or fund looking to throw their money in with what might be the next unicorn on the New York Stock Exchange, but it's wise to be cautious. The old saying "There's a sucker born every minute" is never more accurate than in the technology funding space. The question is, are you a sucker, or are those offering you their cash the ones who are being less than wise?

I am not a banker, nor am I a financial expert. But as an analyst at a major analyst firm and someone who has coached and watched a variety of companies go through this process, I would suggest that, at the very least, I know what *not* to do. And if you remember from the earlier chapters, there is value in that knowledge.

The first thing to know is that the expectations for growth and revenue generation are shockingly high in the technology space. The expected growth rate for a company with VC funding can vary significantly depending on various factors, including the industry, market conditions, the specific startup's business model, and the investors' goals. VC investors typically seek a substantial increase in the startup's valuation over a short period, usually as fast as three years. In many cases, VC-backed companies aim for annual revenue growth rates of 50 percent or higher—and when you consider that the average growth rate of a company is usually less than 5 percent, that 50 percent number shows its teeth.

Mature industries such as manufacturing, retail, and consumer goods tend to experience slower growth rates than emerging or high-tech sectors. In these industries, average growth rates typically range between 2 percent and 6 percent annually. Even startup offerings in those nontechnology markets generally are only expected to grow at a maximum of around 15 percent year over year. Other factors affect that growth and are inherent to different market spaces, but the point is that 50 percent is a moonshot number for anyone to achieve. And remember that 50 percent is the low end of what investors expect. It's not the ceiling; it's the floor!

That expected growth rate may sound reasonable for the VC investors who are offering the cash; they give your company a substantial chunk of investment, and they expect a significant return. Sure, that's fair. But think about it for a minute. In three years, can you guarantee a 50 percent return on a multi-million-dollar investment? With all the moving parts that must be

managed as a company grows, things can quickly get more difficult. A few million dollars in a first round of funding might help
your business pour gas on the fire, but you should know that the
VC investor is expecting napalm on a bonfire, not a few new
embers glowing hotter.

Besides the high expected return, there are other things to
consider when choosing whether to take that sweet VC cash
injection. Here are a few of them:

1. *Loss of control:* By accepting VC funding, startups often give
   up a portion of their ownership and decision-making power.
   Venture capitalists typically require a seat on the board and
   may have a say in important business decisions. Founders
   who prioritize retaining control over their company's direction and strategy may opt for alternative funding sources.

2. *Pressure for rapid growth:* VC investors typically expect startups to grow rapidly. This pressure to scale quickly can lead to
   excessive risk-taking and prioritizing short-term gains over
   long-term sustainability. Some founders may prefer to maintain a steady pace of growth that aligns with their vision
   and values.

3. *Misaligned objectives:* The goals and priorities of VC investors
   may not always align with those of the startup founders.
   Whereas founders may focus on building a sustainable business with a long-term vision, VCs may prioritize maximizing
   returns within a specific timeframe, leading to potential con-
   flicts and divergent strategies.

4. *Financial obligations and exit expectations:* Startups may face
   pressure to achieve specific milestones or pursue an exit
   strategy, such as going public or being acquired, to generate
   returns for their investors. If founders have different plans or
   timelines, they may prefer to forgo VC funding.

5. *Alternative funding options:* VC funding is not the only way to finance a startup. Depending on the nature of the business, founders can explore other funding sources like bootstrapping (self-funding), crowdfunding, grants, loans, or strategic partnerships. These options provide greater flexibility and control over the direction of the company.

6. *Dilution of ownership:* Accepting VC funding often involves issuing new shares, which dilutes the ownership stake of existing shareholders, including founders and early employees. This dilution can reduce founders' financial rewards and control over their startup.

It's essential to know that for every dollar of investment you take, you are trading away a bit of control over your company. And remember, you are diluting not only your stake but also the stake of everyone else who has equity or will receive shares in the future. Funding is powerful if used wisely and cautiously, but it can also be a death by a thousand cuts. Let me explain via two stories of companies I have observed on either side of the funding blade.

I will start with a company that played the funding game right. For privacy, I will call this company ThreatSpike and its CEO Doug. ThreatSpike formed out of Doug's head. Doug ran a small firm that was hacked multiple times, and he was fed up with the endpoint security failures he was exposed to. Doug was naturally a programmer and knew that he could fix the situation.

So that's what he did. Doug sold his small company and used the limited resources he got from the sale, along with a mortgage on his house, to build and launch ThreatSpike.

It took Doug and his brother, another programmer, about nine months to build an MVP (minimum viable product) offering. Following that, Doug and his brother landed roughly half a dozen design partners who tested the software for free and helped ThreatSpike iterate on customer needs. After successfully taking in that customer feedback and refining their software, Doug and his brother converted the design-partner customers to paid customers. They had six to eight paying customers and could show a 100 percent conversion rate, and their customers were thrilled to be referenced, as the ThreatSpike software did precisely what Doug said it would. It stopped threats from successfully exploiting endpoints for customers.

By the end of year one, Doug and ThreatSpike had a well-oiled machine running. But they needed money to keep the grease on the skids and maintain momentum for the business.

Time to get funding.

Doug knew that taking in a seed round—a small early investment round—was possible, as he was in a good market and had precise numbers to show a return and substantial growth. But he also knew that if he took a significant amount of cash from anyone at this point, dilution would begin. In addition, Doug learned that taking in that money would put him and his company on the speed-freak hamster wheel that a VC investor would focus on. ThreatSpike would immediately be on the go-fast track investors wanted.

Doug decided he would focus on getting funding via a technology accelerator funded by a national program. That national program had millions of dollars in a fund set up to build technology-specific businesses and to fund, coach, and launch those businesses into the market as viable organizations upon completion of the program. Doug and his crew at ThreatSpike, now three people (his wife was his chief of operations), dedicated their efforts to getting accepted to the accelerator program. Through their hard work and a series of fortunate circumstances, such as the accelerator opening additional spots for new companies, Doug and ThreatSpike landed in the accelerator program.

Instantly, they had a $500,000 investment round with no dilution and no loss of corporate control. Additionally, ThreatSpike was provided with office space, a travel budget, business connections, and various resources to help the company get to market quickly and efficiently.

Fast-forward a year from their acceptance into the accelerator program, and Doug and ThreatSpike were live. The company grew 50 percent quarter over quarter, and Doug and ThreatSpike now had nearly 100 employees.

Doug and ThreatSpike were valued at around $100 million in less than two years. Now was the time to take actual VC money, as Doug and ThreatSpike were in power. Doug had been fielding calls and emails from VC investors begging him to take a round. But because he had no dilution and an exponentially growing market cap, Doug could call the shots on the funding. He waited another six months, kept ThreatSpike on a solid upward trend, and then decided to take investment. ThreatSpike took a $30 million VC round at the end of year two and was valued at over $200 million. As of today, five years in, ThreatSpike has taken no additional funding and was last valued at nearly $1 billion. ThreatSpike will likely go public soon.

ThreatSpike is a success story for sure, but the success came from Doug being smart and hustling for the company's early growth. Doug figured out the system and used the investment process to his company's benefit. At any point in the company's journey, Doug could have taken a useful amount of investment and followed the same path as other companies. But that was counter to his longer-term ideas and would have put more power in the hands of VC investors who weren't on the ground doing the work with him. Those early decisions made all the difference for his company and his employees.

The power transfer that comes with an investment round must be part of your consideration as a leader. It's worth noting that in early-stage funding rounds, such as seed or Series A, it's not uncommon for VC investors to seek a significant ownership stake in exchange for their investment. The typical stake investors seek in these rounds can range from 20 percent to 40 percent, although it can be higher or lower depending on the specific circumstances. If you have ever watched the show *Shark Tank*, you should get the gist of this.

As a company progresses through subsequent funding rounds and grows, the dilution experienced by founders and early shareholders tends to increase. Each new funding round usually involves issuing additional shares, which dilutes the ownership of existing shareholders, including founders, employees, and early investors.

It's a puddle of water that eventually grows into an ocean of diluted equity, and the only ones with oars and a raft are the VC investors.

ThreatSpike is a success story, but now let me tell you a tale of a business that followed an orthogonal path for funding and has suffered as a result. Let's call this company Xumina. Xumina was much like ThreatSpike in that the founders started the company by solving a problem they faced after being hacked.

Xumina's founders were hit with a nasty compromise and noted that the real problem was that once the hackers accessed their system, they could move laterally without impacting their attack progression. Xumina's founder, DJ, was also a computer programmer and decided he could build a solution that would virtually deploy mini-firewalls on every asset in a digital system. Again, like ThreatSpike, DJ and Xumina's solution worked.

They, too, landed a few early design partners and friendly customers to validate their offering. After a year, half a dozen paying customers were ecstatic about the Xumina solution. One of those early friendly customers was a long-time friend of DJ's who also happened to be the founder of a successful VC firm.

It wasn't long until DJ had a check for $20 million in VC. To get that check, he had to trade three board seats and a significant portion of ownership of the company, but the deal was done, and Xumina was off to the races.

Fast-forward 18 months, and Xumina had grown—along with the early investors' and founders' expectations and assumptions—and was ready to keep growing. At this point, the company could have kept slogging along the way most businesses would, but in the tech space, everything is about speed to market, so DJ's VC buddy and his co-founder convinced him to take another much larger investment round.

Although on the surface all seemed well and good, in reality, DJ and Xumina gained more runway with their big investment round but also gave up a lot to get it. More board seats were gone, and additional equity had to be shoveled around to get the deal inked. If nothing happened in the market, all would be okay.

Well, DJ and his company took that round one month before the known world collapsed on itself from a virus affectionately known as COVID-19. In less than a quarter, the world turned upside down, entire economies crashed, and millions were infected with the disease. Much of Xumina's workforce was either laid off or sick. The hypergrowth of the cybertechnology space hit a literal standstill, and things went from bad to abysmal for Xumina. It wasn't long before the VC investor started asking what was being done with their money, and the board (now composed almost entirely of investors) started to push Xumina to pivot and force growth. All DJ and his founding team could do was try to swim against the massive current of a once-a-century pandemic as the world descended further into cataclysm. Their customer base effectively dried up because although spending increased across the market for cybersecurity, it was mostly from small and medium-sized businesses. Xumina's method of protection was aimed almost exclusively at enterprises, which tended to lock their efforts in place and wait for the tumult to pass.

DJ and his co-founder were effectively removed from their leadership positions several months later. A new Silicon Valley-bred, VC-friendly CEO was installed, and the board voted to take an even bigger investment round to help float the company through the pandemic.

Xumina survived the pandemic, is still in the market, and has finally begun a slow move toward growth. DJ and his co-founder are involved with the company but as far removed from leading the organization as possible. The VC investor and the new CEO are running things.

The funding flip-flops the company ran through as it tried to force growth led to the massive dilution of DJ's and his early employees' equity. The value of their share in the company is roughly one-fiftieth of what it might have been.

Sure, you could argue that DJ and his team got taken by the VC investor, and if they were better businesspeople, things wouldn't have gone the way they did. But I have repeatedly seen this happen in the cyber and technology industry with companies whose founders have swallowed the sweetly poisoned pill of early and easy VC money. The lure of growth at an expedited rate and the potential reward of an early exit often prove too much for founders who aren't aware of the intricacies of the funding process. Typically, technologists and founders of technology companies are not "businesspeople," and they're at a disadvantage in money matters.

Many technology founders learn the hard way that money helps them move fast, but there is always a price to be paid. Early expectations of growth that win investments often don't turn out as hot and fast as the technology space thinks it should. Founders become hamsters running endlessly on a fundraising wheel rather than serving their customers. VC investors and people whose jobs are to raise capital and fund other companies know what they're doing and are very good at it.

Does this story mean you, as a leader, should never take investment money? No. But it's a cautionary tale that we should all heed. If you run your company strategically and focus on practical but realistic growth, the odds are more significant that you will either not need an investment or can grow by "eating what you kill." Like ThreatSpike, you are in the power position and can take the money you need rather than the cash you want. Xumina went sideways because of various factors, but the primary issue was that the founders took money early in their rush to market, which gutted the early equity holders. Yes, the business needed to be fast to gain ground and stay ahead of the competition (so did ThreatSpike). But by not waiting and growing from the ground up, the co-founders transferred their ownership to the VC investor and the board and diluted their equity exponentially.

One thing founders and leaders often forget as they try to grow their company with VC money is that their early employees' equity is also diluted as the founders raise money—in the case of Xumina, the founders' feverish fundraising robbed their early employees of nearly all of their equity value. The math pointed to the company having to go public and land a major IPO event to reward those early employees with a financial windfall—one they deserved, honestly. Imagine being the CEO who had to tell the folks who had been in the trenches since day one, "Sorry, we did all we could to raise money, and part of that meant we lost some of our share value. But hey, we kept growth steady, and the VC investors are ready to give us more to keep the business healthy." How flat and fake must that come across to employees who put their faith, time, work, and hope into a CEO who has effectively gutted their future finances?

Yes, it's a gamble, and yes, the employees know that, but they never wanted to play against a stacked deck. And that's what the CEO does in these scenarios; they let the house dictate the stakes, and the house always wins.

I speak from personal experience here. I was part of a company where I was among the first 20 employees. The company was on a great trajectory, but the CEO and his leadership team sought to put napalm on a bonfire with a VC investment. As things sometimes go, the market adapted, and the business scrambled. Additionally, the CEO turned down a $300 million acquisition offer because "my investors say we are a billion-dollar company." The acquirer's leadership team laughed as they left the room. "Okay, good luck with that" was their only comment as they went out, giggling to themselves. Not long after, the CEO and his VC advisors worked on another exponentially larger investment deal, and the flushing sound got louder. The business was circling the drain faster and faster. More money and chasing the market led to the value of the early employees' stock being worth about as much as toilet paper. I framed my stock certificate and hung the framed document in my bathroom as an emergency wipe in case I ever needed it. To this day, the company is staggering along and still in debt to its funders. Every early employee has left, and the CEO moved to another country.

As a leader, don't start by chasing money that isn't coming from customer acquisition. Land customers and grow from revenue, and then consider a funding round, but only after you have some astute business advisors and lawyers ready to handle all the jargon. Always remember that you, as the leader, owe it to those who have joined you on your journey to keep as much value in the company as possible. VC money is easy to get, but there is a sucker born every minute (and they're counting on that). Don't be that sucker, and don't rob your loyal employees of the outcomes they expect for their efforts.

CHAPTER

9

Don't Be a Mushroom Farmer

My theory on feds is that they're like mushrooms; feed 'em shit and keep 'em in the dark.

—Sergeant Dingnam, *The Departed*

Mushrooms are a controversial food in my experience. There are those who love fungi as part of their diet, myself included. And some loathe mushrooms and think they're "dirt." My kids would fall into that latter grouping. Whether or not you are a mushroom fan, they're useful in various ways. Yes, there is the magic kind that has shown value for treating ailments like depression and helping with other mental health issues, as well as making some music and movies much more engaging. Other mushrooms can be used to replace meat in a person's diet.

Some mushrooms are being used to replace steaks in some kitch-ens. In New York City, I experienced a dessert made from some unknown (to me) mushroom, and it was delicious.

What is interesting about these miracles of the food world is how they're grown. The mushrooms most of us are familiar with are the big white kind that grows in the yard or the basement when we get too much rain or ignore the wife's pleas to de-funk the cellar. But the good kind, the kind we eat, get much better and more attentive care as they grow. To grow a mushroom for consumption, the basics are something like this:

1. Buy a mushroom-growing kit, or grind up some old mush-rooms you purchased.

2. Put the spores and kit items in a cool, dark place.

3. Cover them with compost or other fertilizer-type material (manure works well).

4. Leave them alone and let them grow.

5. Harvest your shrooms and enjoy, or torture those who hate them by covertly inserting mushrooms into their food. (Okay, don't do that, but it's how I got my kids to eat mushrooms in their spaghetti.)

That's a dumbed-down version of the professional way to grow your own edible (food-quality, not stoner-quality) mush-rooms. The most critical thing I have learned about growing your own mushrooms is that temperature and a lack of sunshine matter most. Interestingly, if you want bigger mushrooms, put more fertilizer on the spores and substrate. The darker, colder, and more covered in shit they are, the better the mush-rooms will do.

By now, you are wondering why a book about leadership includes information about growing mushrooms. Well, that's simple. You can grow all the mushrooms you want at home under the sink, in the dark and cold—but don't be a mushroom farmer with your people. To be clear, I don't mean you shouldn't treat people like fungi; I hope that's evident, but why not clarify? A good leader must not treat their people as if they would do well if kept in the dark and cold and covered with bad information. People are not fungi and shouldn't be treated as such.

People want and, depending on what research you read, need to be exposed to light and must be nourished with quality inputs. But in business, leaders often think it's wise or best if they try to mushroom farm with their employees. Leaders have an important decision to make, or there is a critical event on the horizon, and instead of including their people in the process, these leaders keep them in the dark and "feed them shit."

Let me tell you about a time when I was treated like a mushroom and provide insight into how it affected me and the entire company. I will also provide a narrative about one of the most famous mushroom farmers in history, whose actions led to the death of hundreds of innocent people. Seriously, mushroom farming is dangerous.

For my tale, I was working as a consultant to a company lining itself up for an acquisition. The company had been around for a while and, in recent years, had finally shown the type of growth that technology investors and acquirers look for. From day one of the acquisition operation, the CEO and his team of bankers set a tone of secrecy. The group's first meeting in the process was titled "Read in only." In the intelligence community and the military, that terminology is reserved for the most classified of operations. Being part of the team present during the Bin Laden operation required being "read in;" the term is that serious. It was odd to see the same language in a business email thread. That day, the CEO explained his and the bankers' plan to sell the company and repeatedly reiterated that nothing was to "go beyond this room."

Following that initial meeting and email, the CEO and his team became even more insular. The circle of people involved in or aware of the machinations taking place became smaller by the day. A month later, the number of people who had any actual valuable knowledge about the actions taking place or the associated timelines was down to five: the CEO, his lifelong friend and business partner, and the three bankers managing the deal. Even the company's founder, who launched the company years ago and brought in the current CEO to modernize sales efforts, was ousted from the inner circle, as he was deemed likely to talk to others. Would he have talked? Probably; but he needed to speak, especially to those employees who had been with him from day one and needed to know what was happening.

Of course, some degree of secrecy makes sense, and yes, there is always a risk of information leakage putting a deal at risk. And yes, keeping those who often gossip and spill secrets at arm's length is wise. Still, an acquisition is a potentially life-altering activity that can benefit everyone in the company. By setting the tone of absolute secrecy and making it obligatory for the limited few who were "read in," the CEO inadvertently set up a mushroom farm.

An interesting fact about certain mushrooms and fungi is that they're interconnected underground (or sometimes on the earth's surface) by a layer of connectivity called a *mycelium network*. If you've watched the HBO series *The Last of Us*, you've seen humans infected with monstrous fungi operate as a collective when a single twinge is felt along the connected substrata. In a business, when mushroom farming begins, connective tissue or substrata begins to form, proportional to the level of shit being fed to the mushrooms (the employees). And just as the fungi zombies communicate, so do the employees. All it takes is a single twinge along the corporate substrata, and communication spreads throughout the network. One person who wasn't included in a meeting begins to make assumptions about what is occurring, another shroom down the hall hears the conversation in a hallway, and bingo, the twinge becomes a thread.

This communication system won't stop, and the more leadership tries to insulate itself from the rumors percolating among the mushrooms, the more they're mushroom farming their employees. Even if leadership at this point tries to stop the mushrooms from communicating and making their inferences, it's too late. The spores of doubt and distrust are spreading in the air. Anything that comes from the mushroom farmers—the leadership—will now be seen as just more manure to be tossed onto those being farmed. It's an entirely avoidable vicious cycle.

As just another mushroom at the company I was consulting with, I was in the dark, and my distrust for leadership's sharing of news was greater by the day. Worst of all, the other mushrooms in the company leaned toward me to get details and insight from leadership, which I did not have. This helped to further brew distrust and sowed the spores of doubt at every company level. No one at the company believed that I, as an outside agent, did not have unique insight into the machinations taking place. Why would the leadership pay me and not tell me everything? I found myself an isolated mushroom in a bed of shit, trying to reach toward the light.

Fast-forward nine months; yes, it took that long to complete the acquisition. To this day, I think a combination of the market taking a dive and general buffoonery was to blame. Regardless, the CEO was finally ready to announce that the deal was done and he had sold the company. He expected rapturous exaltation but instead got only muffled clapping and doubtful glares. Because of the clandestine nature of the operation, many long-term employees were just learning that a sale was taking place. Most of them had zero insight into the fact that their careers in the company were not only in jeopardy but, in some cases, gone, as the acquirer was planning to trim the fat post-acquisition. And because only the "read-in" group had been privy to the sale, many of those long-term employees never had a chance to renegotiate their equity and stock options. More than a few had been at the company since its inception but walked away with only a few thousand dollars in payouts, while the CEO and his bankers got seven-figure paydays from the deal.

The CEO and the bankers combined forces with the acquiring company's leadership to host a celebration shared across the company's virtual meeting system. It was one of the most hollow and shallow parties I have ever seen. The mushrooms who had been in the dark for so long were suddenly thrust into the blinding light of corporate shenanigans and stared, angry and depressed, as the moneymakers clinked glasses.

Did the deal get done? Yes. Did some folks make money? Yes. Was it a win for the company? It depends who you ask. For the many mushrooms, it was nothing more than a transaction that gave them a pittance for an outcome. It was a great day for the few at the very top of the mushroom-farming operation. Following the acquisition, the company looked like a sinking ship with rats bailing out of every porthole. The CEO, who had promised the acquirer that "everyone would stay," was left holding the bag as 30 percent of his employees left within a month. No one wanted to be loyal to a leadership team that left their employees in the dark when it mattered most. And certainly, no one wanted to rely on a leadership team that had made a deal to sell the company with full knowledge that many long-time employees were getting financially shafted.

The CEO and his team could have approached this entire endeavor differently. From the start of the operation, they could have advised the whole company that a plan was being put in place to potentially sell the company very soon. They could have sent nondisclosure agreements to the employees specific to this transaction, which would have helped legally enforce discretion. The CEO and his bankers could have advised the employees monthly about the major milestones and status of the deal. And finally, they should have worked with the long-tenured employees to negotiate additional options, because they deserved it. Doing all or some of those things would have shed light and engaged the employees in the deal. Yes, there would be risks, but there always are. And it's much better to have an informed person discussing what is taking place than to have a gossip sharing incorrect information with others.

Another example of mushroom farming comes from a close look at the *Titanic* catastrophe. If you are unfamiliar with the *Titanic*, the summary is that the "unsinkable" ship RMS *Titanic* sank. What does that ship's sinking have to do with mushroom farming? As the typical business case, it was all about leadership and communication.

The captain of the *Titanic* was Edward John Smith, aged 62 years at the time of the *Titanic's* sinking. Smith had been commodore of the White Star Fleet since 1904 and had more than four decades of experience at sea. On the night the *Titanic* hit the iceberg that ultimately sank it, the ship received at least five documented reports of ice before Smith decided to change course (The National Archives, n.d.). Captain Smith was not ignoring the ice warnings; he was simply not reacting to them. Ice warnings were warnings a ship sent to other ships, saying it had seen ice at a certain location. Captain Smith decided not to slow the vessel despite reports of ice. He was a forceful sailor, known to push his ships hard in certain conditions, and it was not uncommon for captains to sail into regions with ice at full speed (21 to 22 knots, in *Titanic's* case).

On the night of the *Titanic*'s sinking, Captain Smith decided to leave the bridge during the most crucial part of the voyage, when the ship was transiting the known ice field, to attend a dinner party (Wilkinson & Hamilton, 2011). He normally took meals in the dinner saloon in his cabin, but since he was retiring after this voyage, he decided to rub elbows with the elite passengers in first class and build his future notoriety in high society. He left the party early to talk to his team on the bridge and then retired to his cabin at around 9:20 p.m. Captain Smith chose to go to bed early even as the ship was moving at top speed through the ice field, wherein other ships had reported sightings of icebergs.

Captain Smith knew he was gambling. He had also commanded the RMS *Olympic* when it collided with the HMS *Hawke* while leaving Southampton harbor (Wilkinson & Hamilton, 2011). Excessive ship speed and the limitation that the ship's transit speed placed on the bridge crew's ability to react were among the causes of the collision, just as with the *Titanic*'s situation. In simpler terms, Captain Smith knew from experience that a bridge crew on a speeding ship could not respond fast enough to a potential threat to avoid a collision. In the case of the RMS *Olympic*, the hazards and risks were clearly visible, but speed was the factor that led to the inability to react quickly enough. Captain Smith was aware that speed in an ice field was a risk factor, yet during the voyage of the *Titanic*, he decided to go to sleep and rely on his bridge crew's experience and skill.

According to a post-incident report, the SS *Californian* was less than 20 miles from the stricken *Titanic*. The *Californian*'s Captain Stanley Lord had ordered his ship to stop its maneuvering due to the risk of icebergs. Earlier the same night, Captain Lord had ordered his radio operators to communicate to nearby vessels about the increasing threat of ice collisions.

His operators received a response of "shut up" from direct communication with the *Titanic* (Clarke, 2012). Possibly, that response was guided by the ship's bridge crew, who had tired of the warnings while their captain was intent on steaming full ahead.

At 11:40 p.m. on April 14, the *Titanic* struck an iceberg at full speed (Daugherty, 2020). Captain Smith reportedly appeared on the bridge deck minutes after the impact and was informed by his fourth officer that the ship had hit an iceberg but there was "no damage." Reportedly, the ship's designer, Thomas Andrews, traversed the vessel and found the damage extensive. *Titanic* was designed to float with four fully flooded compartments; Andrews found at least five flooded (Daugherty, 2020). Estimates at this point in the calamity are that *Titanic* had about 90 minutes before it sank to a watery grave in the icy Atlantic. But Smith and his leadership team became focused on dealing with the need for rescue by other ships, as they knew there were not enough lifeboats for all the passengers and crew. Not for at least another hour did Smith and his bridge crew call for the deployment of the lifeboats they *did* have. Deploying lifeboats as the ship was already listing heavily made the endeavor to save lives even more precarious and likely added to the loss of life.

Over 1,300 passengers and crew died when *Titanic* sank. During the follow-on inquiries and testimonies after the event, crew members noted that Captain Smith "kept to himself" and "had full faith in his skills." Rightfully so: with 40-plus years at the helm, Captain Smith should have had faith in his skillset, but it was folly for him to decide that only he knew what was right for the ship as it traversed an ice field. At least three different officers questioned him about the speed of the vessel and "whether it's wise to continue at the maximum speed," only for him to shrug off those questions, attend a dinner, and go to bed on the very night an iceberg would rip through *Titanic*'s hull.

These failures, of course, are on top of the mushroom farming wherein the White Star Line leadership and Captain Smith were fully aware that there were fewer than one-third as many lifeboats onboard the ship as would be needed should a cataclysm occur. None of that risk was effectively communicated to the passengers or even the most senior leadership, as the ship was "unsinkable." How many passengers and crew would have stayed away from the doomed voyage if they had known of the lack of lifeboats onboard? "How much revenue would we lose if that fact were communicated?" was almost certainly the thinking of the executives at the White Star Line when the calculus was done. To them, it was apparently worth the risk of human life to have the passengers and crew in the dark and keep the numbers up and the business side of the company steaming forward. The leaders of the White Star Line company and Captain Smith were mushroom farmers of the highest order. Unfortunately, their decisions and the lack of shared information and decision-making led to a catastrophe of historic proportions.

What's the best thing about knowing what a mushroom farmer is? You don't have to be a mushroom farmer. You can easily choose not to be. All that is required is to treat your employees and stakeholders as people, not fungi. Not being a mushroom farmer doesn't mean you as a leader need to jeopardize your decision-making process; you can keep your cards close to the vest if you think it wise. But you should take the opportunity to share what you can with those who need to know and deserve to be included. People are better at keeping secrets when they realize there is no real secret to share. When you bring them into the light and stop treating them like mushrooms, you will find that your employees and stakeholders are more engaged and willing to collaborate with you.

Additionally, those mushrooms can focus on what is needed for the collective good when they know why and how the efforts underway benefit them. Share the light. Feed them insight. Trust them as you wish to be trusted, and have faith that you did the right thing by hiring those people in the first place. You will be much better off as an open and honest leader than another mushroom farmer shoving shit on those who deserve to be treated as anything but mushrooms.

10

Choose Your Horse Wisely. . .

A thoroughbred racehorse can go from 0 to 40 in a matter of three strides. It's exhilarating; the feeling of power underneath you is incredible. I love to learn what makes a thoroughbred tick.

—Chris McCarron

When I moved to Virginia, seeing all the horse farms was terrific. One thing you find out about horse farms is that although the owners want to educate and help folks learn how to ride, a horse farm is a business first. And just like everyone else in business, horse farm owners are always looking for a way to gain an edge over the competition. Owners of horse farms will do anything to own the best horse they can and, at some point, sell that animal to whoever else is willing to buy a new pony.

There was a horse farm down the road from me whose owner typically had horses used for jumping and pageantry, which is a solid business. He was content with the money he was making, as he was selling horses that were pretty good at what most folks bought those types of horses for. He got married, and his new wife thought there was a way to do more business and sell horses that were not just for pageantry but also for work on cattle farms. What she meant by "work" was that ranchers would use those horses to do things like cut cattle, herd cattle, and generally be cowboy horses.

That concept makes sense and sounds like an excellent way for a horse farmer to do more business. The problem is, horses typically only do one or two things well. You can't take a pageantry horse and put a different saddle on it, and suddenly it's a cattle horse. That's not how these animals work. To complicate things further, the owner's wife wanted to add thoroughbred horses to their stock—horses bred to do one thing and do it to the best of their ability. So, the couple dove into this plan. Fast-forward a year or two, and they had bought five or six adult thoroughbred racehorses they intended to sell as potential cattle horses. His wife wanted to flip the horses: buy them low and sell them high as next-generation cattle horses. Seriously, that's what they told me.

What must be understood about a thoroughbred racehorse, though, is that it is a giant ball of muscle with only one thing on its mind: running as fast as possible in a straight line.

Thoroughbreds run in a straight line, and that's about it. They aren't good for much else. They run as fast as their muscles will move them, and they would run until they fell over if they didn't know there was a finish line. Pageantry and cattle horses, on the other hand, are content to do whatever they're told: jump around, stomp their hooves, cut cattle, and move cattle when needed. A good cattle horse or pageant horse is a Swiss Army Knife; it can perform a much broader scope of activities than a racehorse can. Most of these types of horses are pretty chill, as well. They're relatively relaxed, they do a job, and unless they are actively on a job, they eat grass and crap wherever they stand. You can pet them. Kids can get near them. Regular horses are a lot like family SUVs, you could say.

Thoroughbred racehorses, however, are Corvettes. They are high energy, high maintenance, and essentially bonkers if they are doing anything but running. Racehorses bite people. They gnash their teeth and chomp at their bit constantly. Racehorses will smash down fences and run over a rider or owner if that person isn't careful. And they are always at high speed. Thoroughbreds never calm down, and you can tell how amped up they are because their eyes are usually wide and their nostrils flared. A slight sound can send one rocketing off into the distance. They are fast, but they are nuts. And they are bred to be this way. Generations of breeding have genetically hardwired these beasts to be on edge constantly. They are not to be owned by the faint of heart or the inexperienced.

The horse farm's theory behind this strategy was that if they had these high-energy, super-fast, sports-car-type horses, they could gain an advantage over others by selling them and breeding them for the cattle industry because they would be quicker, better, and faster than legacy cattle horses. But when the couple took those horses to market, they found out very quickly no one in the cattle industry wanted thoroughbreds. No one wanted racehorses around their cattle, and no cowboys wanted to ride them. They were too risky. Those ranchers and riders knew that racehorses were crazy, and they wanted nothing to do with them.

At the market, the thoroughbreds always moved at Mach 3, and riders were tossed right and left. No matter how hard a potential buyer tried to direct them, all the thoroughbreds wanted to do was go straight. Not a good thing when you need to cut cows from the herd. Having invested hundreds of thousands of dollars in thoroughbred horses, the owner wondered what to do with his herd. All he could do was keep them in the barn, let them out in the pasture, and hope those insane horses didn't hurt themselves or someone else as they bounced off the fences like giant hairy ping-pong balls.

The worst thing that could happen would be for the horses to waste away. Sadly, that's what happened. The owner couldn't sell them back to the racing community because they had been tainted and not used in the way they were bred. Those thoroughbreds no longer had any value in racing because they had been out of the circuits for a while, and their ability to race was in question. Added to that, the racing community would not allow them to breed. The owner's horses were now tainted thoroughbreds, and no racehorse owner would allow them to mate with their pristine stock. These horses were essentially useless and had no value in the jumping and pageantry, cattle, or racing industries.

So, what to do with them? The only answer was to let them mill around. The horses went from inside the stockade to out in the pasture to back in the barn, all day, every day. In a matter of months, all the horses got lazy and fat, lost muscle mass, and went insane. They had nothing to do. They tore up fences, destroyed property, bit people, and chewed through barbed wire. Anything you can think of that a horse should not do, those horses did. It was a nightmare. The owner had to feed them and watch his horse farm flush money down the toilet to keep those animals alive and cared for. It was sad to see, and unfortunately, all he could do was wait for the horses to age and die. His heart broke because he was watching beautiful animals go from being in tiptop shape and examples of genetic perfection to being fat, lazy, relatively useless, insane animals that served no purpose.

What can we take away from this horse tale? The long and short of it is that trying to gain a competitive advantage by obtaining an animal that may be better in one particular way isn't always the best approach. If the organization isn't ready for everything such a high-performance asset might bring, things go bad. Fast. Although this was a narrative about horses, the same thinking should apply to our businesses and our thinking as leaders.

As a leader, you may consider bringing on a thoroughbred to help build, run, or market something within your organization or company. To be clear, it is not a horse but someone who exemplifies a racehorse or thoroughbred level of output. That makes sense: high-performing individuals, whether in sales, marketing, or any other organization area, can bring tremendous value. But you must be careful to understand that those high-performing individuals are most often good at only one or, at best, a few things. And thoroughbreds must be used for what they were "bred" to do. Anything else is folly and will only harm the organization, and you will be doing a disservice to the thoroughbred.

A racehorse must be aimed in a particular direction and allowed to run. Thoroughbreds, human or horse, must be allowed to run as fast as they can toward a goal. That's how a person gets to be known as a thoroughbred in the first place. That's why you hire them. You seek out those individuals because you know they are high-performing and high-energy and will deliver results if allowed to run. If you brought those individuals, those thoroughbreds, into your organization and chained them to the floor, they would not do well.

Individuals who operate as thoroughbreds are usually good at only one or two things. They are fantastic at sales, or they are the best at marketing and growing an organization from the inside. They do something of immense value, and they do it well and within a confined vertical; you need a track, if you will. When you acquire the services of a thoroughbred, you are responsible for caring for and feeding that high-performing individual. If you do not care for them properly and allow them to do what they are best at and do so at their speed, they will get frustrated.

They will go a bit insane, and they won't like being in your organization because you are robbing them of their potential and their opportunity. If you're going to bring a thoroughbred into your organization, make sure you have room for them to run. Empower those individuals, and loosen the reins so they run as hard and fast as possible and deliver for you. They know what they should do and are chomping at the bit to do it.

As the guy with the horse farm learned, you cannot take a thoroughbred racehorse, throw them into a cattle ranch, and expect them to perform like all the other horses. They will need to figure out what to do in an unfamiliar space. That lack of direction and clarity of purpose will make them nuts and dilute their value to the organization as they flounder when they should be running at high speed, growing, and solving problems. Bringing a thoroughbred into a business is not far from this reality.

Suppose you want to bring a thoroughbred individual to your organization. You should understand that there will be additional costs and other requirements to keep that individual happy and performing at their highest level. Perform the calculus on whether you can do all these things well before you seek out such an employee. I can tell you from personal experience that when you find a thoroughbred, if you provide an opportunity they think they can provide value in, they want to do it. They want to run that race. They want to go for it if they see an opportunity and do so with full force and conviction.

Unfortunately, an organization often finds the thoroughbred individual they are seeking and brings them into the company before they have a complete plan for how the company will enable that new horse to succeed. It is not wise to put a thoroughbred horse on a small track and say, "Go slow." If you find those individuals and bring them in, be sure the track is wide, and they have room to run. The last thing you want is a crazy, frustrated, malnourished thoroughbred romping around your organization, trying to figure out what the hell they are supposed to do.

I have seen this in various organizations. Most tech companies are always looking for an edge on the competition, just like every other business and like the horse farm I discussed at the beginning of this chapter. They seek out any advantage they can find, often leading them to look for a high performer to bring into the stable.

I was working with a company seeking a stellar performer to be their sales leader. This company was young, had VC funding, and was looking to grow as fast as possible. The executives thought that if they could bring in a high-performing sales-leader-type individual with a history of winning and high growth, that thoroughbred could help their organization grow exceptionally fast. Logically, this made sense. However, the organization itself needed to be at a higher level of performance before they brought in a thoroughbred.

Against advice from various sources, they sought an individual with that type of history. The person they found had delivered incredible results and sold hundreds of millions of dollars of software at various companies. So the company made a great offer and promised this thoroughbred all the room to run he would need. But they brought this person in, put them in a stall, and said, "Go slower. Go sell software, but do it so we can keep up."

The new company's leaders failed to understand what they should do with this thoroughbred. The company leadership should have considered that this horse had been operating in large organizations for a long time, where he had room to run and all the support he needed to work as a thoroughbred. He was cared for, and his reins were lightly handled as he ran like lightning, always moving forward at breakneck speed. Big companies could let that happen and were ready for any bucking that might occur should they need to rein him in.

In this new company, the leaders had been brought in to help grow something, but they also needed to learn how to develop the organization to match a thoroughbred's speed. Organizations with the heft and infrastructure to support this individual could run a race like no one else. But this new business, a small company, wanted a 10-ton steam hammer in a space that could only accommodate a jeweler's hammer.

It took a little while before the thoroughbred realized he was in a space where he wouldn't do well because he was trying to sell software for a company that couldn't keep up with him. Things quickly went awry. In less than 90 days, the thoroughbred lined up significant accounts and was holding millions of dollars' worth of contracts the new company could not execute.

What does that failure to execute do for the thoroughbred individual? First, it makes them question their decision to come to the organization and why they are risking their reputation for a business that can't keep up with them.

Second, it causes frustration for a thoroughbred because they are doing what they were brought in to do, but no one else is. The thoroughbred is delivering just as they should and functioning as the high performer they were hired to be in the first place.

Third, it destroys the business's ability to continue to sell or grow in line with its expectations based on the use of these types of thoroughbreds. The organization thinks it can grow and scale up because of the superstar it has brought in, but it needs help to keep up with the thoroughbred. Leadership looks stupid when one person is outperforming the rest of the business.

Finally, this approach causes future customers to question the company's ability to deliver. The organization that hired the thoroughbred will wind up apologizing for its inability to fulfill contracts. When the organization grows and fixes those problems and fails to deliver, it will return to the contacts the thoroughbred provided and try to reengage. However, knowing the company didn't deliver the first time, the contacts are unlikely to give it another chance, especially if one or more of those contacts happen to be thoroughbreds themselves.

Much like horses, thoroughbreds in the business world travel in herds. If you see a group of mustangs roaming across the prairie, those are fast horses that all coordinate and collaborate to stay alive. The same thing happens with business thoroughbreds. They know each other and talk to each other. If something goes sideways for one thoroughbred, the rest are fully aware of what happened and why, and they will talk about it. And if your organization has put a thoroughbred in a position where they can't succeed, you had best believe the others in the herd will know that something has gone wrong and who is responsible.

The organization I was working with saw their sales go nowhere. Nothing happened that was of any value. The thoroughbred was going crazy trying to figure out why the organization was doing this to him and why the company was willing to risk its reputation on something that would fail. The meetings this individual attended were increasingly corrosive. Things began to spiral downward at an exponentially increasing rate. Meanwhile, the board needed more evidence that things were improving. Fast-forward one more quarter, and the thoroughbred turned in his papers and said, "I quit." Now the company founder and executives had to find another person to hire, which further delayed progress and caused more problems. The thoroughbred was frustrated and was sure to inform every other thoroughbred he knew in the space that it was unwise to work for that company. Any thoroughbred buyers were advised not to buy from that company. The water trough had been poisoned.

As a leader, you want to grow your business and gain every tactical and strategic advantage. One way to do that is to hire individuals who will bring their thoroughbred spirit and energy to your organization. But be cautious about the thoroughbred you go after. Once you've decided to buy that horse, so to speak, and you put them in the arena, it's too late. In some rare cases, a thoroughbred may have the drive and wherewithal to drag an entire organization toward success, probably kicking and screaming. But often, the new hire will find things exceptionally frustrating and will not do well. And the organization will suffer for it.

I have been one of those thoroughbreds. I hate to write that, as it makes me feel like a braggart, but the story is instructive here. I was hired to come into an organization and build their security practice. When I was recruited, I was told that the entire leadership team "expected me to go fast and do big things." The CEO and CTO wanted "disruption" and "business dynamism." It was all word salad. What they really wanted was someone on staff with a bit of credibility in the security space so they could leverage that name to build their brand. There was not and never would be any actual initiative to evolve the company or "do big things." They hired me, walked me into the barn, stuck a bit in my mouth, and tried to keep the reins tight as they fumbled about in the saddle.

It wasn't long before I went nuts. Everything I tried to bring into the organization was met with "Whoa, slow down. We don't work that way." Or "We'll think about it." It was to be business as usual, except with a prize pony prancing about the paddock, and I was that pony. I hated everything about it, and that dislike and disenchantment spilled into the workspace. All I could do was look for the nearest fence to jump and try to find a way out of the barn. It sucked. My attitude went downhill; depression even set in for a while, and I became increasingly isolated: no one wanted to continue to hear me gripe and paw at the ground in frustration. The day I quit was one of the best days of my professional life.

It's fine to try to gain an advantage whatever way you can, including seeking out thoroughbreds. But as with everything in business, taking the time to realize the delivery needs and the organization's ability to execute is the primary concern. Seek a thoroughbred "in the wild," and ask them what they need to be successful. You can't talk to a real horse, obviously, but you can ask a high performer what they must have to do well in your business. Make sure you can provide them with what they need and understand the realities of having a performer like that in your arena. If you can use them correctly, they can be exceptionally valuable. Great things can happen; races can be won.

But never take on a thoroughbred racehorse when you really need a cattle horse. A thoroughbred needs to run as fast as possible toward the finish line and must be allowed to do so. It must have only minimal control applied to it so it can perform at the high level for which it was born. The cattle horse buckles down, goes to work, and performs well, which may be exactly what you need.

11

Don't Lose Perspective, and Never Let Your Ego (Or Title) Write Checks Your Ass Can't Cash

Social media has made too many of you comfortable with disrespecting people and not getting punched in the mouth for it.

—Maria Higgins

There is a great scene in the Frank Miller comic book series *300*, which was made well before the Zach Snyder movie (just in case you were only familiar with the movie and the many Spartan thongs therein). At the beginning of the story, a messenger from the Persian army rides into the Greek capital and presents King Leonidas with the heads of previously conquered rulers.

The messenger then takes it upon himself to dictate the terms of King Leonidas's compliance with Xerxes, the Persian king. "Earth and water is all we require," he says smugly. King Leonidas takes a few seconds to consider this offer and promptly kicks the messenger into the nearest bottomless pit. The movie makes this scene fun to watch and incredibly dramatic, and you get the point: the messenger would not be delivering any more messages, ever.

In this scenario, there is something we should learn. The messenger was proud of his king and overly confident in his positional authority. He thought he could ride into the Greek capital with brashness and threaten the king of the Spartans, who were known far and wide to be the pinnacle of warriors at the time. The messenger relied on his experience with lesser men rather than being cautious, thoughtful, and respectful when confronting someone he knew *of* but was unfamiliar *with* personally.

The messenger did not take time to consider what might happen when he arrived, and he certainly had not done his homework on what to expect from King Leonidas. It cost the messenger and his men their lives and launched the 300 on their march to the Hot Gates to confront the Persian army. The messenger made a fatal error and let his hubris, his ego, write a check his ass would never be able to cash, and he paid for it.

This type of interaction, although without the Spartan thongs and swords, happens all too often in the business space. By not keeping things in perspective related to our past experiences, our persona, others' perception of us, and the people and situations we encounter, we risk putting ourselves in precarious positions. It's always wise to treat every interaction with people as one where both your and their perspectives matter. No matter how many heads you carry when you ride in to meet with another person, it's unwise to think they will be impressed (much less intimidated) by your historical exploits.

Also, the odds are that if you're reading this book—and I hope you're getting something out of it—you work in the technology space. That's good. Technology is one of the best areas where someone can grow into a great leader. All too often, however, I have found that technologists for some reason strive to be something other than what they are.

Many technology leaders have an odd desire to be Navy SEALs or Army Rangers or to compare themselves to combat operators. Sure, there are possible correlations between being in combat and going above and beyond as Special Operations and other military members do and leading a company or organization in business. As a business leader, you could compare yourself to a leader who runs an organization in the military.

But those two things are inherently different. Let me provide you with some context. Take a moment to consider the most junior person serving in the military. Most of them joined directly out of high school. Then they went through a 12- to 16-week boot camp, followed by a year-long or multiyear advanced training program. After that, they were sent to a unit where they began doing their job, typically what most people would consider a regular job. But unlike the typical civilian job (especially most technology leadership jobs), military members are always on call.

Furthermore, military members sign a contract saying they are willing to put their lives on the line. They agree that they will risk their lives if needed to serve those in this country. I doubt you're asking yourself or your employees to agree to die if need be to deliver software on time and on budget.

A military job may be simple, but every military job requires a spirit of service above self. The junior service person does this willingly, knowingly, and all while earning what most would consider a comically low salary, especially compared to technology-sector salaries. Service members must also deal with deployments, where their life goes haywire. A deployment upends the whole of their existence. If you've never served in the military, imagine having everything you do turned on its head logistically, physically, emotionally, financially, and organizationally, and going to a foreign country where you could lose your life. A deployment typically lasts 6 to 18 months. During this time, even a very junior member not directly engaged in combat operations must work long days, usually well over the 12- to 16-hour mark. They will eat shitty food, experience a never-ending lack of sleep, and always be aware of the risk of death. And they will do all this for a lower salary than a fast-food worker. They also don't live at the Ritz Carlton. Things are even more complicated and stressful if the service member is part of a Special Operations or combat-focused job role.

Those in the Special Operations Forces (SoF) community are the most motivated, qualified, and trained individuals in the fighting force. A Navy SEAL trainee runs 20 to 30 miles a week just back and forth to the chow hall. Marine Raiders ruck march hundreds of miles with the weight of a human slung across their shoulders. Army Rangers endure months of training in hostile environments that even animals avoid. The training alone for a Special Forces operator includes hundreds of hours of repetitive training, long days and nights, constant risk of significant injury, and months away from loved ones and home. Many of my best friends are either active duty or retired Navy SEALs, and their stories about their deployment and training sound worse than any support deployment that most military personnel have ever been on. They operate at an entirely different human level. Again, although it's hard to run a technology company, keep your perspective. None of us are subject to those miseries, and none of us will run into a firefight over who ate the last bagel in the company pantry.

It's possible someone from the SoF community is reading this; if you are, thank you for your service, and God bless you.

But if you're not an SoF operator, remember that you're not deployed in a combat zone, putting your life on the line to serve a customer. You're not at risk of being blown up while driving to the chow hall. There is no day you can't roll out of bed, decide you've had too much, and lie back down and take another nap. No one at your company works 24 hours a day, seven days a week. Don't treat your business or employees as if they were SEAL Team Six.

Silicon Valley CEOs and technology leaders from across the nation try, sometimes internationally, to embrace a bit too literally the ideas and concepts these military leaders espouse. I have attended many leadership meetings where Silicon Valley groups considered taking the SEAL team challenge or offering team-building events that mirror SoF training.

The saddest sight I ever saw as a technologist was when a startup leader in San Diego decided to have his development team go to Coronado for a "SEAL Day." The day started at 0430, most of his folks were late, and things went downhill from there. No one wanted to jump into the 65-degree surf or make "sugar cookies" (where you cover yourself head to toe in sand and water) and do calisthenics for hours on end. When presented with the chance to fire live weapons exactly like those they played with virtually during their lunch-break "Modern Warfare" sessions, the team members quickly discovered that real guns are hot, heavy, and loud. It took fewer than 50 rounds for the team to decide they had had enough of "SEAL Day." They bitched and moaned incessantly, and before lunch, the entire development team packed their bags, flipped the boss the bird, and left. He stood there, profoundly unimpressed, and was handed a bill for $15,000 for a half-day clusterfuck that had only succeeded in making his team hate him and question his sanity as a leader.

It makes sense to bring in the learning, education, and ethos that some organizations at the tip of the spear hold so dear.

However, it's unwise to try to treat your people or yourself as if
you were members of one of these elite units. You are not. The
military leads people differently because, at some point, life is literally on the line; and when lead is flying, it's okay to engage a
subordinate with a more direct and vicious tone to get things done.
There is a reason: when you're deployed and something goes
wrong, a leader can grab you by the collar and physically move you
to where you need to go because if they don't do that, you might
get shot. There's never a reason to do that in the technology space.
You don't need to treat your people the way military leaders treat
their people. The best thing you can do to align with some of a
military organization's principles is to engage in conversations
around the ideas and concepts those units leverage. But always
keep it real. Remember, you will not die if you don't deliver a piece
of technology to a customer, and neither will the customer.

The best military leaders I have ever been around, including
those engaged in combat operations, were able to get your attention by how they acted and conducted themselves during incredibly stressful times. You knew those leaders were in command
because of their calm nature when things went bonkers. You
could see that they were managing themselves and the situation.

It's not only corporate leaders who can lose their perspective
and let their ego get them in trouble. Even one of the greatest
military leaders in history lost his perspective—and it cost
him dearly.

General George S. Patton, known as Old Blood and Guts, is
renowned as one of the greatest military leaders in American history. He led troops in bloody battles for decades and was instrumental in the Allied victory in World War II. But his hubris and
a momentary lack of judgment, combined with his ego and a loss
of perspective, negatively impacted his future.

That incident, where General Patton struck a service member, occurred during World War II. General Patton was leading

the U.S. Third Army to great successes in the European theater. In August 1943, during the Sicily campaign, Patton visited wounded soldiers at a field hospital in Nicosia, Sicily (D'Este, 1996). There, he encountered Private Charles H. Kuhl, a shell-shocked soldier suffering from battle fatigue. Reportedly, Patton believed Kuhl's condition was a sign of weakness and lack of courage, which greatly angered him. Kuhl had been on the front lines and was physically uninjured at the time, but his nerves and his mind were fractured. In today's parlance, we would say he was afflicted with post-traumatic stress disorder.

In a moment of frustration and anger, General Patton struck Private Kuhl across the face and shook him by the shoulders. Patton's actions shocked those present and caused outrage among soldiers and officers alike. Striking a subordinate, especially one who was wounded and vulnerable, was a breach of military discipline and against the values of the U.S. Army. As news of the incident spread, it reached the higher echelons of command, leading to an investigation. Patton faced severe criticism for his behavior, and many people up and down the chain of command called for his removal. Instead, he was reprimanded and required to publicly apologize to Private Kuhl, the soldiers present, and the entirety of the Third Army (D'Este, 1996).

While he was still revered for his military prowess and strategic brilliance, the fact that he had struck a vulnerable and wounded soldier led to questions about Patton's temperament and ability to handle the stresses of command. As a result of the incident, Patton's superiors became more cautious about his behavior and limited some of his duties. While he retained his command of the Third Army, he was often kept away from the media and was given assignments off the front lines to avoid further incidents or negative publicity. The soldiers he met with were less likely to be honest with him about the issues they faced, and his senior leaders were concerned about his place in the Army. It took one moment for a career to be called into question.

In today's world, almost everyone working in the technology space is a keyboard warrior. Many young people who enter technology and become leaders have spent their lives behind a keyboard.

The keyboard provides a person with a buffer: a safety net that keeps them away from human contact if they want that to be the case. These leaders use their keyboard and the internet's safety to talk down to people and treat them poorly because they know they don't have to be physically close to the individuals they are interacting with. They know they can sit there and be assholes and get away with it because nothing bad will happen to them.

A keyboard warrior can be as mean as they want via chat, Slack, email, or phone and say whatever they choose. If human resources becomes aware of it, the resulting reprimand will be nothing more than a letter of warning or an HR person saying "Stop doing that," especially if the keyboard warrior is the founder or CEO. What HR person would want to counsel or reprimand the person who hired them and is issuing their paychecks? The weak effect of HR punishments has made individuals far too comfortable with being keyboard warriors and treating others poorly because they know they are safe if they stay behind that keyboard.

I have seen many CEOs in the technology space talk combatively to employees via a Slack channel or email. However, when it comes time to confront those individuals in person, that same leader will cower and find a way to smile and make things pleasant. Don't be that leader. Don't be a person who hides behind a keyboard and talks a big game but whose badassery crumbles in the physical presence of an individual you insulted.

As leaders, we should always know that our job is to work with and serve others. It's not to denigrate people and bring them down. The need to build others up does not mean you must constantly be effusive in your praise, but you should be cautious about the words you use and how you talk to people, even if it's from behind a computer. Sooner or later, you must be in a room with those on that Slack channel. At some point, you will have to face whoever you sent that nasty email to.

How will you handle that interaction? If you're a keyboard warrior, nothing good will come from derisive messages. You will wind up facing whomever you derided, and when you do, one of you will look away; one of you will yield their gaze. And when that happens, the person who did not yield is in a powerful position. If you're the CEO or the boss, and you're the one who breaks your gaze and looks at the floor because you realize you were a jackass, you have now lost that individual's respect. As we know from earlier chapters, respect is a crucial currency you can't afford to lose.

Once I was consulting for an organization and ran into one of the most egregious examples of a keyboard warrior I've ever known. I consulted with the organization by trying to sell to customers and grow the business. The leader of this organization was notoriously hotheaded and very much a keyboard warrior when it came to Slack messages and emails. Sometimes he was also corrosive on phone calls with people because he knew he was beyond their physical reach.

This individual thought of himself as a Navy SEAL leader even though he had no military background. But he was the spear's tip; he used those words in multiple meetings. In his mind, he was engaged in combat as he did the work; he was there to bring people along and lead them through the charge. He worked hard. He was someone people respected for his ability to get things done, but other than that, he was a walking contradiction regarding what he thought he was and how he thought he acted.

Ironically, even though he thought of himself in military terms, he didn't have a spirit of service. He was a former sales executive who had found a way to weasel into a CEO gig. He liked making money and was willing to do anything to make more of it.

I had heard his method of leadership on calls with others in the organization, and it genuinely concerned me; however, as a consultant, I never dealt directly with someone in a leadership position or served in one myself. I was there for advisory purposes and to offer insights, not to put my boots on the ground. All I could do was take notes and try to make others aware of the situation. But when it came to one issue we were dealing with, I'd had enough. It was my time to chime in and bring something to the CEO's awareness. The CEO, however, was unhappy with the issue I brought to light. In this instance, we needed to deal with everything that was going wrong with a program the CEO had implemented himself. He was angry at the failure of execution and was trying to shift the blame to others. My point to him was, ultimately, that the buck stopped with him. But my assertion was not something he was willing to accept.

The conversation quickly turned combative.

The CEO asked the other team members to drop off the call and said he wanted to "handle this with me." Okay. I knew what was coming, I was not scared of a fight, and I was more than willing to engage in verbal combat with anyone at any time. That's just my persona.

I was fully prepared for verbal fisticuffs. But that was different from the way this conversation went. The CEO lost his mind when the other leadership team members dropped off the call. He slung profanity and told me I was no longer worth engaging in the contract. He made a few threatening remarks, even commenting on my abilities to perform as a husband and father. Then he paused, expecting me to retort similarly. But I maintained my composure and let the dead air hang on the line. Because of COVID, this was a Zoom call, and I could see him via webcam. He did not have the luxury of hiding behind a faceless phone call and could also see my posture and gestures. We were in a stare-down.

While he was still seething, I stared at the camera and said, "Are you done?"

He looked quizzically at me.

I said, "What's your address?"

The CEO asked me, "Why?" I said, "I want your address because you live somewhere near me."

"Well, I don't want to give you my address. What would you need my address for? We're on a call right now."

My response to him was simple: "If we're gonna have a conversation like this, I want to be within striking distance of you. No one will talk to me like that and tell me these things and call me those names and do it behind the keyboard. If you wanna talk to me like that, you're going to do it within striking distance."

He asked, "What do you mean by striking distance?"

"Within my reach. Physically is what I mean. Right now, you're a keyboard warrior, and if you want to have it out, let's have it out. But not over Zoom."

His response was interesting. His eyebrows lifted, and he sat back for a second.

He said, "I don't think I've ever had anyone say they would be willing to come to my house and kick my ass."

My response was, "Brother, today's the day."

That calmed the situation immediately.

I don't know whether this guy had never been challenged before, and my goal was never to challenge someone physically, but he quickly understood that I was willing to risk physical pain to confront him. He understood that his actions, activities, and language would not be tolerated, were we in the same physical space. He also admitted that he had never heard the term "keyboard warrior" before.

The entire conversation shifted and became something much more constructive. I won't tell you we had a great relationship. If I'm honest, I still don't like this guy, but I did gain respect for him because he was willing to listen for a moment after he stepped back and learned that some people would not allow anyone to disrespect them. He had lost his perspective and let his ego write a check his ass nearly had to cash. His actions and style hurt our collaboration and poisoned the well.

If you're unwilling to get your ass kicked and endure pain, don't be a keyboard warrior with other people. As I said at the beginning of this chapter, we aren't Navy SEALs, and the people we are trying to lead aren't active military engaged in combat operations.

Always be thoughtful and respectful, listen, and treat your people as they deserve to be treated. If you're unwilling to be physically present with someone and risk an ass-kicking, don't abuse them from behind a keyboard.

Take a moment, step back, and take a deep breath before typing or speaking what's on your mind. Don't be a keyboard warrior.

12

Get Past the Fatal Funnel

What's the fatal funnel? . . . It's a narrow confining area that offers little-to-no mobility and often provides no cover or concealment.

—75th Ranger Battalion Training Document

A doorway is nothing exciting. There isn't much to one. A doorway is a simple transition point between two spaces. That's it. You go through it and move to the next space. We do this many times every day, and it's no big deal. However, a doorway takes on a much heavier meaning when you are in a combat situation. A doorway becomes a fatal funnel.

When you join the U.S. military, but before you go to war, you are placed in various training scenarios. Prior to going to war in Iraq, the United States fought wars in jungle environments or large open battlefields, and the military trained its warriors accordingly. The Iraq war forced the U.S. military to rethink and revamp the way it trained and fought because of the change in the environment we were fighting in. In the Iraqi war, the battlefield was an urban hellscape. There were no open areas, and every door, window, and building was a potential shooting position or kill house.

Iraq was an entirely new battlespace. Combat operations in Iraq were nearly completely within cities, and the enemy was an insurgent force. Every house and every door in those houses had to be opened and cleared during engagements with the enemy. It was a hazardous place to be, and the method of engaging the enemy fundamentally differed from past combat for our armed forces.

Clearing a house is a terrifying ordeal. Imagine playing hide and seek with an overly sugared-up six-year-old who also happens to have grenades, trip wires, and automatic weapons at their disposal. Then play hide and seek on unfamiliar turf where the hider has a home-field advantage. You begin to get the concept. The only way to deem a house clear is to search it, floor by floor and door by door. Each turn around a corner or walk up the stairs might result in a volley of fire erupting in close quarters.

When conducting a clearance operation, the one place you don't wish to spend any more time than necessary is a doorway.

The doorway is the fatal funnel.

If you stop or delay your movement, that transition space will be your grave if an enemy is on the other side. You can't see past a door and can't effectively fight from a doorway. You must get past the doorway fast and effectively, and you want someone following right behind you as you enter the next room.

You need them following you because you will clear a specific room sector, and they should follow you and clear the rest. If that next person isn't on your hip as you move through the doorway, the odds of you being shot and killed increase, as you won't have time to clear the entire space yourself, and the bad guy hiding in the opposite corner will light you up as you clear your corners.

But a doorway is often a point where progress stops for the untrained and inexperienced.

That terrifying fatal funnel before you dares you to ask, "What if I don't go through?"

"Can't we just shut the door?" "Can't I poke my head in and see what's there?"

You must go through, do so quickly, and be prepared to do violence as you move. You can't just shut the door and move past it without clearing the room.

A bad guy might be in there who will pop out and shoot you in the back as you move onward. And no, you shouldn't poke your head in and look, because you can't shoot back via your face. You need that weapon to go first, and you need to lead with the barrel to effect action if required. Sticking your head in or trying to peek into the space cautiously will only help the enemy dial in on you and shoot you in the face as you stand in the doorway and delay entry. When things go wrong in a house-clearing or search operation—and they often do—you will be closely engaged with someone who wants to end your existence on earth. You will be in what is typically known as CQB (close-quarters battle).

The concept of the fatal funnel isn't limited to military operations and has also been adopted in law enforcement settings to refer to building searches or room-clearing operations. Law enforcement officers are also trained to be cautious and vigilant while approaching and entering confined spaces such as hallways or doorways, as these areas can pose significant risks due to their limited access and potential for ambush.

Why are you reading about house-clearing and combat operations in a leadership book, in particular a book about what a leader shouldn't do to be as effective as possible? Just like in combat, there are places you don't want to stop progress, and you don't want others to stop there, either. Key areas exist within daily and long-term business operations that can funnel you into potential risks, such as delayed sales, missed projections, and inaccurate planning for a growth trajectory.

You must know how to deal with those fatal funnels and what you should consider conceptually to get past them. Just as in a house-clearing operation, to be effective as leaders, we must know how to observe and orient ourselves and when and how to move past the riskiest areas. Let's discuss this concept.

The term *fatal funnel* underscores the importance of situational awareness and proper tactics when navigating confined spaces and chokepoints, reminding individuals to exercise caution and take appropriate measures to mitigate the risks associated with such spaces. There are a few key points to learn to be as effective as possible during operations in and around a fatal funnel:

1. *Minimizing exposure:* Doorways are high-risk areas where individuals are highly vulnerable to enemy fire or ambush. By clearing the doorway swiftly, the time spent in the fatal funnel is minimized, reducing the chances of being targeted or engaged by adversaries. This is also applicable in a business context. You don't want your weakness and potential vulnerability exposed by simply getting stuck in the "door." Keep moving, and reduce your risk exposure at all times.

2. *Gaining tactical advantage:* Speed is critical in gaining a tactical advantage during fatal-funnel operations. Rapidly clearing a doorway allows the assaulting team to maintain momentum and surprise, catching potential threats off guard. It enables the team to swiftly enter the room or area beyond the doorway, gaining control and maintaining the element of surprise. Being first to market is always a good thing. When you have an opportunity to do that, execute your move smartly and smoothly. This keeps the competition off guard and buys your company interest and demand in the market.

3. *Reducing collateral damage:* Clearing a doorway helps minimize the risk of collateral damage. When a team is in the fatal funnel, any shots fired by adversaries or team members can potentially hit individuals outside the doorway or in proximity. Swiftly clearing the doorway reduces the risk of unintentionally hitting friendly forces or bystanders. Collateral damage occurs in the business context when the failure to execute affects other indirectly impacted business units. It might affect the HR team if you fail to hire the right people or the marketing team if they constantly have to readjust their go-to-market based on execution issues.

4. *Maintaining initiative:* Speed is essential in maintaining initiative and dictating the flow of the operation. By clearing the doorway rapidly, the assaulting team can control the pace and tempo of the engagement. Movement and initiative prevent adversaries from establishing defensive positions or coordinating effective countermeasures. In business, we should always determine where we can vector resources to increase wins. Growth can feed growth, and success is the best drug; leverage your initiative, and gain when you can to drive outcomes.

5. *Limiting opportunities for adversaries:* Clearing a doorway denies adversaries the opportunity to react effectively. Rapid movement and the element of surprise make it harder for them to establish a defensive posture or engage the assaulting team. It reduces their ability to gather information, coordinate with others, or execute an effective counterattack. Protecting your intellectual property and competitive advantage is a key need. Be cautious about your offerings and open source initiatives and social media connections. I have seen many companies lose initiative and success because one developer left company secrets or source code exposed on the Internet.

Being good at room entry and house clearing means you can move and decide quickly. You are aware of the present risks but committed to eliminating hazards and threats as you proceed smartly but aggressively.

You will not stop and stall as you transition through the fatal funnel, and you will not allow others to do so either, as that is where they're most likely to start a permanent nap. No one goes in alone, and no one enters a room solo.

You will always be first in or follow the point person closely as they clear a room so you can clean up and defend them if they miss a threat. Finally, constant progress is necessary. Constantly progressing on the end objective prevents stagnating and slowing down. Focusing on only allowing communication and clarifying risks and objectives will aid your organization The last and possibly most important thing to know about clearing a room or house is that if you stop or stumble as you pass through a doorway, the person behind you will either shove you through it or push past you as they move onward. There is no stopping once the first step is taken through the transition point, as you never want to surrender area that you now own. I have seen many trainees stop or stumble at a doorway, only to have a more experienced operator shove them to the ground as they maneuvered into the room.

Okay, that's enough fatal-funnel education and training. The takeaway is that speed and movement are critical. Not getting stuck in the fatal funnel is also crucial to business success.

In business, the fatal funnel is often its go-to-market and marketing and sales alignment. The fatal funnel isn't a widely recognized term or concept in marketing and sales. However, some aspects of marketing can be analogous to a funnel where potential customers move through various stages of the buyer's journey. Let's explore these stages and how the concept can be applied metaphorically.

Typically, most marketers and sales leaders see the funnel as simply a means to orient around the leads coming in and how they're being used. This methodology aims to get as many leads as possible at the top of the funnel. Hopefully, with enough squeezing, sales will pop out on the far end. In the middle of the funnel is the land of the lost. It's where leads stall out and potentially die. Those leads came in hot from an outward or inbound marketing initiative, but due to various circumstances, they are now in limbo. If the doorway you are trying to get through is customer acquisition, the transition should be as smooth as possible. You should reduce friction often and repeatedly for the buyer.

In this context, the first phase of the fatal funnel is customer awareness (Keller, 2007). At the top of the marketing funnel, the goal is to attract the attention of potential customers and create awareness of your brand, product, or service. This stage is the widest part of the funnel, where a large audience is exposed to your marketing efforts. It's not necessarily a fatal stage, as it primarily focuses on generating interest and capturing attention. But what *is* fatal at this stage is allowing the noise of the market and your competitors to drown out your voice in the space.

In a fatal funnel in a military or law-enforcement context, the goal is to minimize exposure. However, you want to maximize exposure in the marketing context and ensure that the customer fully knows the benefits you offer and the problems you solve. Many in the industry call this *thought leadership*. Exercising thought leadership isn't wrong, but remember that although you want that customer to acknowledge your presence, they need to move onward in the funnel. You want them to stay energized at this stage and not become enamored with your thought leadership alone. You want sales and acquisition, not just acknowledgment. In this step in the funnel, you should be focused on the quality of content for the potential buyer as well as the clarity you're offering that your business is the one that solves the customer's problems. Additionally, you want this stage in the funnel to be where potential buyers most notice your organization.

Your thought leadership and go-to-market strategy at this stage should prompt the potential buyer to act, not just think. They're already thinking about the problems they face, so they're considering a solution in the first place. Your content at this stage should continually educate but always motivate the buyer to move onward. If your content is doing nothing more than letting the experts on your team feel intellectually validated and praised, find other content. At this stage, it's easy for a lead to go stale as customers are inundated with material from various companies and thought leaders, all championing their own solutions. If you wish to move your leads beyond that first chokepoint and save them from the land of the lost, focus on the value of your offerings and their alignment with those potential buyers (Shah, 2014).

The second step is the consideration stage, where potential customers move down the funnel, inching ever closer to a buying decision (Keller, 2007). In the consideration stage, they evaluate different options and compare alternatives. This phase could be seen as the funnel narrowing, as customers become more selective and focused on a smaller set of choices. Their goal at this stage is to rule out solutions and offerings that don't meet their needs. There may be some risk for businesses in terms of competition, but this stage usually doesn't represent a fatal situation.

Often, analysis paralysis sets in during this second stage. People see the objective and know they should get past it, but they overthink and stop their progress. That only benefits your adversaries—the competition—and stalls your momentum. Allowing a customer to stall at this point can be fatal for the future deal you hope to close. Much as with the house-clearing move-through-the-door directive, at this stage you must work to "push" customers to transition. The longer they consider alternatives, the less the consideration works in anyone's favor.

In this second stage, you want to reignite the interest of leads who have been in limbo. The top of the marketing funnel is usually always active, but the middle of the funnel, where leads go cold, is a point of critical failure that you can turn into an area of reinvigoration. However, simply presenting the same material that was hot to leads that are now cold won't work. You need new material and adapted tactics to drive those leads to move further through the chokepoint. Demonstrations, trial software licenses, and active engagement can help greatly at this stage and will let those leads know that your organization values their potential business (Shah, 2014). Rewashing and reusing already-shared content will not prompt action. Be more active, and help the potential buyer experience, not just understand, the value your offering provides.

Third, we have the decision stage (Keller, 2007). The decision stage is the final step of the marketing funnel, where the potential customers you have educated and convinced that your competitors aren't value-aligned are ready to make a purchasing decision. This is the narrowest part of the funnel. It's the last few inches of the transition beyond the chokepoint of consideration.

Here, the buyer's choices are limited to a few alternatives. If you allow the customer's progress or thinking to stop at this stage, the deal will die in the doorway. At this last critical step, you must help your customers move well past the kill point by whatever means necessary. To stall here is to die. You also want more than one decision-maker moving through the door at this stage. In a house-clearing scenario, there is confidence in someone following you into a room to clear it; there is also confidence in the buyer's perspective if the decider isn't alone in that decision-making process. Have multiple champions on the buyer's side coming through the door in succession. A herd mentality and safety in numbers help make decision-makers feel justified in the research and selection process. Everyone feels safer when they aren't the only ones through the door, clearing the room. And just as in a room-clearing operation, they may need to be urged through the transition. This can be done in various ways, but all of them require you and your team to stay engaged and focused as you aid the buyer in the final steps.

As with a house-clearing operation, you aren't done once the transition finally occurs. You must move onward, cautiously caring for and feeding your newly acquired customer. Your team should ensure that they're happy and healthy and are willing to act as a potential funnel filler for your business. Having a happy newly acquired customer add a referral customer expedites the move through the funnel for your business. It greatly minimizes the time and effort required to move that new lead through your funnel.

When it comes to the marketing and sales realms, the worst thing that can happen is for the funnel to get clogged. Just as in a house-clearing operation, stalling at a chokepoint means terrible things are about to happen. As a leader, you should be constantly analyzing your funnel for efficacy. When you have identified obvious areas of degradation, correct them and rework the approach until the transition from each phase smooths out. The less friction the buyer experiences through the totality of your funnel, the more repeatable and predictable positive outcomes become.

13

Don't Chase Unicorns

There are some who went off in search of unicorns but found only rhinoceros.

—Laurent Binet, *The Seventh Function of Language*

First of all, let's clarify what is meant by a *unicorn* in this context. We often hear about technology companies being unicorns when they reach the billion-dollar valuation. Most of those unicorns experience exceptional valuations that are speculative at best. That valuation is a gold sticker for the founders and investors involved in getting those companies to that level, but the actual value of the companies usually isn't a billion dollars. Various business journals list roughly 260 members of the Unicorn Club in the technology space.

The horn those unicorns wear is an emblem of their achievement of the magical billion-dollar mark, but when one does the math, the magic quickly burns away like so much cheap smoke at a Vegas off-strip magic show. Stanford professor Ilya Strebulaev applied a correct economic model to the unicorns listed on Crunchbase and found that, on average, the shares of those companies were valued at 60 percent above the fair market price. So, more than half the unicorns in the stable are just horses with funny appendages.

Startup success and failure are common in all industries, especially the tech industry, due to its dynamic and competitive nature. Many startups, including unicorns, face challenges; but some overcome them and continue to thrive, while others may not be able to sustain their initial success. Market conditions, competition, mismanagement, and other factors influence a company's fate. Unicorn status does not prevent common market variables from making a business fail and will not insulate a previously successful founder from floundering.

Seeking to become a unicorn company can be tempting for entrepreneurs due to the perceived prestige and financial success associated with such a status. But it's unwise for companies to prioritize being a unicorn, for several reasons:

1. *Misaligned focus:* Striving to be a unicorn can shift the company's focus from creating genuine value for customers to pursuing high valuations at all costs. This misalignment can compromise product quality, customer satisfaction, and long-term sustainability.

2. *Excessive risk-taking:* Companies fixated on unicorn status may be more likely to take on excessive risk to achieve rapid growth, which can lead to reckless decision-making, overspending, and bankruptcy if things don't go as planned.

3. *Unsustainable growth:* Rapid and unsustainable growth driven solely by the pursuit of unicorn status can lead to operational inefficiencies, strained resources, and an inability to manage the company effectively.

4. *Valuation expectations:* Unicorns are expected to maintain high valuations, which can put significant pressure on the company's performance and increase the need for continuous fundraising, leading to potential dilution of ownership. Investors may also look at how much money a company has raised as a signal of its success, when in fact it shows the opposite.

5. *Market realities:* Not all industries or business models can support unicorn valuations. Striving for unrealistic valuations can lead to disappointment and disillusionment when faced with market realities.

6. *Neglecting profitability:* Companies chasing unicorn status may prioritize growth over profitability, leading to extended periods of losses and a lack of focus on building a sustainable and profitable business.

7. *Market saturation:* The Unicorn Club has become crowded, leading to increased competition and potentially inflated valuations. Not all companies can achieve such high valuations in a competitive market.

8. *Limited exit opportunities:* Achieving unicorn status can limit exit opportunities, as only a few potential buyers or IPO markets may be capable of absorbing such large valuations.

Instead of focusing solely on achieving unicorn status, companies are often better off prioritizing creating value for customers, developing sustainable business models, and building profitable and scalable operations. While rapid growth and high valuations can be positive outcomes for successful startups, they should result from a well-executed business strategy rather than being the primary objective. A more balanced approach that considers long-term viability and customer satisfaction is likely to lead to more sustainable and successful outcomes for companies in the long run.

Consider three unicorn companies that experienced stratospheric growth and exceptional valuations, only to collapse spectacularly: Jawbone, Homejoy, and Quirky.

Jawbone was a consumer electronics company known for its fitness trackers and Bluetooth speakers. Despite achieving unicorn status, Jawbone struggled to compete with other wearable tech companies and eventually collapsed. At one time, top-tier venture capital firms Sequoia, Andreessen Horowitz, Khosla Ventures, and Kleiner Perkins Caufield & Byers, and then a sovereign wealth fund, invested hundreds of millions of dollars in Jawbone, lifting its valuation to over $3 billion in 2014. The company didn't realize it was quickly outpaced by its competitors—Fitbit, Apple, and Google—and ignored market indicators to its detriment. Jawbone (originally named Aliph-Com and then Aliph) was once a company that sold "America's favorite Bluetooth speaker": its Jambox speaker product lineup. Jawbone wasn't the first to enter the Bluetooth wearable space, though, as Motorola had already leaped into the Bluetooth headset arena and was seeing solid success. Motorola's headsets were more utilitarian than fashion accessories and were mainly used by government and police organizations. So, Jawbone introduced the idea that Bluetooth headsets could be practical and fashionable for the masses.

When Jawbone introduced the Aliph Bluetooth headset in 2004, it was met with significant praise. The headset offered "noise shield" technology that had been approved by DARPA (the Defense Advanced Research Projects Agency) (Voss, 2018). This headset laid the groundwork for the Bluetooth headsets we see in global use today.

Moving into a new decade, Jawbone saw significant company growth and secured nearly another quarter of a billion dollars in funding. The company introduced its fifth Bluetooth headset, the Jawbone Era, and its first Android app (Voss, 2018).

The year 2011 also saw Jawbone's focused attempt to break into fitness tracking, which would play a major role in its failure. It introduced its UP series of fitness trackers, popularizing the idea that you could track your heartbeat and health via an accessory. The Jawbone UP was announced in July and became generally available in November 2011. Public reaction to the UP was extremely positive. Yet for no good reason, Jawbone began another round of fundraising, which kicked off in February 2014 and added another $250 million to the company's bankroll.

During this time, things started to take a turn for the worse for Jawbone, as Fitbit's health tracker grew in popularity and began to steal significant portions of Jawbone's market share. By November 2015, Jawbone's market share in wearables dropped to just 2.8 percent of the market, leading to company-wide layoffs (Voss, 2018).

It all came crashing down for Jawbone in September 2016 when company insiders indicated that there was almost no product inventory left on shelves and that Jawbone could not pay its customer service agency. In July 2017, Jawbone decided to shutter options and liquidate its assets.

After seeing so much initial success, and with so much money in the till, how did Jawbone go wrong?

When Jawbone launched UP3 in 2014, a flaw in its first product forced it to miss the ever-important holiday shopping season. That lack of execution, combined with reviews indicating an imperfect product that didn't accurately measure a wearer's heart rate, hurt Jawbone's launch in the wearable fitness market. In 2015, when Apple introduced the Apple Watch, it was too late for Jawbone to claw back its lost market share. By 2016, Fitbit, Xiaomi, Garmin, and Samsung had all eclipsed Jawbone in the health-tracking space.

Once the initial glow of the original UP subsided, all the money in the world couldn't help product delays and quality assurance issues. Of course, Jawbone hoped that a premium price tag for its UP3 would help recoup some of its costs, but at $179.99 on release, the premium price didn't match the feature set.

Jawbone failed for three reasons: betting everything on its fitness lineup, moving away from its core businesses, and raising too much money. In the third case, all the cash and the associated VC "guidance" led the company to focus almost entirely on the fitness tracker space. Finally, as the company's troubles mounted, it went dark across its customer service space, leaving customers with nowhere to go for repairs or technical support.

Homejoy also appeared to be on the glide slope toward total success, only to implode just as it peaked.

Homejoy was one of the first platform companies to disrupt the home cleaning market. It aimed to use algorithms to connect homeowners with cleaners and schedule cleanings from the comfort of an app. Homejoy raised $40 million from sources including Google Ventures and Max Levchin, PayPal's cofounder (Farr, 2015). Nevertheless, the company was shut down less than two years later, becoming a cautionary tale for other companies seeking to attain unicorn status.

Homejoy's failure was attributed to losses from high customer acquisition costs and poor customer retention, a strategy focused exclusively on quick growth, competition, and poor worker retention. At the time of Homejoy's launch, a legacy cleaning company typically charged an average of at least $85 for a 2.5-hour house cleaning. Homejoy, however, offered new customers a promotional price of $19 per cleaning. While many platform companies have subsidized products and services (or offered them for free) to fuel growth, Homejoy's promotional price led to substantial losses, since 75 percent of its bookings came from those discounts alone.

Homejoy's growth-focused strategy might have worked if Homejoy had been able to retain customers, but most customers never used the service again. After all, who wants to pay the full cost of a cleaning and a subscription fee when you can just get one nearly free cleaning and go on with your life? A third-party analysis showed that only 25 percent of customers used the service after the first month, and fewer than 10 percent used it after six months (Farr, 2015).

Homejoy's focus on growth also led it to deprioritize technical issues with its app, such as a glitch in the algorithm that didn't provide cleaners with sufficient time to go from one house to another, making them perpetually late to appointments. Pressure from investors led Homejoy to expand too quickly and incur substantial costs. At one point, Homejoy was operating in more than 30 cities, including New York, London, and Berlin (Madden, 2015). The company's focus on speed and continual quick growth caused it to neglect basic supply-chain and operations requirements. Homejoy ultimately collapsed because it failed to deliver on its value proposition.

Quirky is another dead unicorn added to the pile of Silicon Valley failures. Quirky was a platform for inventors to submit and develop their ideas into consumer products. It filed for bankruptcy in 2015 amid financial difficulties and faced criticism for its business model. The invention platform had, as many would argue, all the factors for a huge success:

- A charismatic founder
- A huge user base that loved the product
- A mission to optimize the process of inventing and patenting physical products
- Massive backing from investors like Andreessen Horowitz, Kleiner Perkins, and General Electric

Still, Quirky didn't sell enough products. The company managed to burn through $185 million and a billion-dollar-plus valuation in venture capital and was forced to file for bankruptcy only a few years after opening its doors (Mann, 2015).

Quirky was founded in 2009 by Ben Kaufman, who was only 22 then. Kaufman had already worked on two other companies, Kluster and Mophie. Quirky was a community-based platform for inventors. Any inventor could pitch their product ideas, which the community voted on. The winning products were then designed, patented, manufactured, marketed, and sold by the company to retailers. The inventor received recognition and about 10 percent of the profits (Lagorio-Chafkin, n.d.).

A lot of ink was spilled in the forums about whether the community voting system was efficient or too democratic. When it comes to business models and monetization, expertise is vital. Having an army of amateurs approve hundreds of solutions that were often unscalable and lacked clear product market fit turned out to be a bad idea that led to a financial death spiral. Countless ideas were brought to market that didn't satisfy clear market needs.

Quirky built more than 50 products annually—the company produced around 400 significantly different products before it shut down (Lagorio-Chafkin, n.d.). Everything in Quirky was designed for speed, prioritizing quantity over quality. After the company launched a hardware product, it made hardly any iterations even when there was huge potential and room for improvement. The firm simply moved on to the next big thing. So rather than having a few solid products with great market fit, Quirky produced many crappy products with minimal market fit. Clearly not the best approach for any business.

Quirky's website was a catalog of all kinds of random products. The company had a confusing brand identity, which is a big problem for building brand loyalty. In Quirky's case, the branding strategy was built around the inventors rather than the products. Quirky wasn't establishing itself as a brand; it was creating a fragmented cadre of inventors who used Quirky. It turned out customers were more interested in purchasing valuable products than reading the touching stories of the people behind them. Wanting quality products from sellers: who knew that was a thing, right?

So, what's the takeaway from looking at these dead unicorns? They didn't fail because they lacked funding, super-cool leaders, sexy products, or a legitimate market. They failed because they were focused on being unicorns rather than growing smartly and delivering for their customers above all.

Quirky was hell-bent on democratizing the invention process and forgot that people want quality products, not quantity. Homejoy thought it could run the market on a long-established service offering by massively undercutting the existing pricing model. It might have worked if the company had remembered to always deliver service and that if an app is key to delivery, it had better work. Jawbone took in money at every turn and quintupled in size in a matter of months, all while trying to build technology that would rival much larger players. Jawbone wasn't satisfied with a great Bluetooth headset; it had to "own the fitness tracker space." That space was still nascent and undeveloped as a consumer market, but Jawbone dove in headfirst; its investors wanted a quick return on their investment. Speed-focused leadership and never-quite-enough bank accounts weighed Jawbone down, and the company lost focus and didn't deliver or even care enough about customer satisfaction to keep support lines open.

If you need more proof that the backers of many unicorns aren't concerned about the company's customers or the leadership's execution, consider WeWork, a mega-unicorn that hit over $40 billion in valuation, only to die a fast, miserable death. The ambitions of Adam Neumann, the company founder, were as ridiculous as his persona. "Rather than just renting desks," *Fast Company* reported, "the company aims to encompass all aspects of people's lives, in both physical and digital worlds." That messianic idea included expanding the WeWork model to residential housing and education. Before Neumann started the company, he envisioned "WeSleep to WeSail to WeBank." WeCult should have been next on his list (Zeitlin, 2019).

Everything went wrong for WeWork soon after it filed documents for an initial public offering of shares. Six weeks later, Neumann voted to remove himself from the CEO job and gave up his majority control of WeWork's stock. The company's proposed valuation fell by over half in less than eight weeks, and the IPO was halted. The failed IPO and the company's subsequent takeover by SoftBank, its largest investor, were triggered by the public exposure of long-known insider information. WeWork was losing massive amounts of money, primarily because of inflated projections of the size of the market for shared office space. Neuman estimated this at over $3 trillion globally, which was wildly optimistic. WeWork estimated that market opportunity by imagining everyone sitting at a desk in the United States as a potential "member." Globally, in non-U.S. cities with WeWorks, the estimates applied to anyone with an office job. WeWork's corporate culture and strategy were also completely locked into Neumann's and his family's bizarre ideas and whims on top of their bonkers market and business estimates.

Neuman left WeWork and moved to start another, similar company, receiving funding from the same groups that watched WeWork burn cash by the billions. Neuman's new company, called Flow, has already received $350 million in funding from Andreessen Horowitz for his upcoming rental real estate venture, also called Flow. The investment puts Flow's valuation at over $1 billion (unicorn status again), and the startup has not even launched yet. Neuman also received $70 million for a Blockchain-based carbon credit platform called Flowcarbon. The ashes of WeWork are still smoldering, yet investors and VC bros are ready to throw more money at a clearly failed leader. Do you see the insanity there?

The backers of these startups are focused on juicing the valuation of their investments into companies. Those investments are business decisions, so the logic of investing in them to achieve quick growth and big unicorn wins makes sense. But it's important to recognize their focus. The backers of those funds and VCs aren't concerned about the other intricacies of the company. No VC or hedge fund manager will lose sleep over the people who must be laid off or care about the second mortgage the owner took on their house to keep the company afloat. If the company gets to unicorn status fast and they win, great. If it doesn't, oh well; they budget for those kinds of losses.

Companies that achieve unicorn status usually don't keep that gold sticker for long. Most fail, and it's estimated that as many as 9 out of 10 unicorns devalue quickly after achieving that goal, as they lose focus or are victims of the market outpacing their growth.

There are many more people in the world who start, nurture, and grow highly successful companies that will never be unicorns. And that's perfectly okay. The desire to be part of the Unicorn Club isn't a good area for your focus. Getting that elusive $1 billion valuation isn't why you started a company, I would guess. In my experience, very few founders and leaders start their business to achieve unicorn status; rather, they want to fix a problem (Brown, 2018). And no customer really cares if they buy quality solutions and products from a unicorn. Customers want their problems solved by businesses that value them as customers.

A successful business can manage external disruptions and withstand market turmoil. Doing so necessitates focusing on cash flow, building revenues, and ensuring that expenses are under control. Doing the basics right repeatedly should be a focus of any solid business, not achieving unicorn status at all costs. Investors will find and underwrite companies built on sound business practices.

Valuation alone doesn't mean much. While the value of a company may make it a unicorn, there is no tangible mountain of gold on which the founders can sit and sneer at the market. Most of the time, entrepreneurs agree to onerous terms to achieve a unicorn valuation. Any new investor coming into future funding rounds or an eventual IPO for a unicorn must radically discount any previous valuations, as they know they're speculative at best.

The most valuable companies last a long time and are leaders in their markets because they continually deliver for their customers. Not because they joined the "tres commas club," as the VC bro from the hit show *Silicon Valley* says about being a unicorn. Harley Davidson, Amazon, Ford, and a long list of other companies have well exceeded $1 billion in actual dollar value, but they didn't do so because of their dedication to being a unicorn. The older companies didn't even have that mark to aspire to when they came on the scene. Those successful companies had leaders who saw that they could solve a customer's problem, and they dedicated their efforts to doing just that over the long haul. Focused and customer-oriented leaders who care for their employees and business operations become unicorns if they want to, but they may not even care if they hit that magic mark. Real value is built over time, absent outside investment and decoupled from any social desire to have a horn stuck to the founder's forehead or get the approval of bankers over customers.

Being a leader of a company in the technology industry (especially cybersecurity) affords massive opportunities for those who venture to build something. But because technology is dynamic and growth can be exponential, founders and leaders often become enamored with the quick attainment of "value" rather than delivering actual value. Don't fall into that trap. Keep your focus and your company's focus on the work you do and the value you bring to your customers. If you get to be a mystical horned beast, great. If not, you'll still have a thriving business, happy customers, engaged employees, and no unicorn shit to step on in your office.

CHAPTER

14

Microscope, Telescope, or Mirror?

It's not what you look at that matters, it's what you see.
—Henry David Thoreau

When you look through a microscope, you can see the details. Electron microscopes can see down to the tiny structures of whatever is in the viewfinder. These powerful analytic devices can manipulate wavelengths of light and harness the power of the electron to provide the viewer with unique insights into previously unseen materials. Were it not for the invention of the microscope, our society would never have achieved the innovations we have in medicine and material sciences and other genuinely groundbreaking discoveries.

While the microscope sees tiny hidden items, a telescope looks ever onward and outward. The James Webb Telescope, or JWT as it's called at NASA, has the power to see the universe's formation. This fantastic technology is orbiting our sun, gathering infrared images via a six-meter primary mirror. JWT will study every phase in the universe's history, ranging from the first luminous glows after the Big Bang, to the formation of solar systems capable of supporting life on planets like Earth, to the evolution of our solar system. This telescope can see beyond the formation of time as we know it and is already sending back detailed pictures of planets far beyond our solar system.

But do you know what both those fantastic tools contain that allows them to be so valuable? (Actually, I've given the answer already.)

Mirrors. Yes, telescopes and microscopes have mirrors within them. In fact, they contain more than one mirror. Each mirror helps enhance the scope's capabilities, and neither would work without mirrors. In both telescopes and microscopes, mirrors play essential roles in the optical system to gather and focus light, allowing us to observe distant objects (in the case of telescopes) or tiny details (in the case of microscopes).

In most reflecting telescopes (Newtonian, Cassegrain, etc.), the system's primary mirror is the largest. It's usually concave (curving inward) and placed at the back of the telescope's tube. The primary mirror collects light from the distant object being observed. The light collected by the primary mirror is reflected toward the secondary mirror, which is usually smaller and flat or slightly curved. The secondary mirror reflects light at a 90-degree angle, directing it through a hole in the primary mirror toward the eyepiece or camera. In many microscopes, especially older designs, mirrors direct external light onto the observed object. These mirrors can be tilted to adjust the illumination angle, which helps achieve proper lighting for the specimen. Mirrors in microscopes are used for illumination purposes, while the primary role of mirrors in telescopes is to collect and direct light from distant objects.

What do microscopes, telescopes, and mirrors have to do with leadership, especially technology leadership? The short answer is that most technology leaders spend far too much time focusing on the details and analytics they see in the eyepieces in their scopes and far too little time looking into the most valuable piece of glass they own: their mirror. And just as the mirrors in those different scopes can be adjusted for differing views, technology founders and leaders often ignore the need to adjust their focus based on what they need to see.

Most technologists are far too focused on the intricacies of how things work—the minutia of their offerings. As these technologists move into leadership positions, either via merit or simply because they built whatever thing they are selling and their investors think the founder should also be CEO, they remain too close to their technology while seeking to look into the distant future simultaneously.

That might sound confusing, but let me expound on the issue. How many times have you seen or read about a technology company founder who is also a CEO or CTO *and* a true visionary? Technologists who are also company leaders who have the capacity to be both simultaneously are few and far between. Often, that technology founder is, in truth, better suited to focus on the technology they have brought to market. They are usually mired in the details of what makes their technology as innovative as they think it is. If they looked in a mirror and genuinely asked themselves, "Am I the right person to run this business as well as build this technology?" the answer would frequently be, "Nope."

In most cases I have seen, technologists are better suited to be a company CTO, not a CEO. That might be hard to hear, but look in the mirror and ask yourself, "Am I CEO material? Do I want to run the business side of this company? Am I ready to do the things that have to happen to make this corporate machine run smoothly? Can I handle those needs as well as the technology innovation and vision side?" If there is any hesitance in your answers, then seriously consider not being (or even trying to be) the CEO. A CTO is still a leadership position and is critical to the company's success, but as a CTO, you can leave the business side of things to the businesspeople. Many technology founders never look in the mirror and realize they are better suited to focusing on their passions: building and deploying technology. We—I am including myself in this group—aren't business leaders, and that's okay. We don't have to be, to be successful.

Consider the case of Elizabeth Holmes of Theranos. She was lauded as a visionary and seen by the Silicon Valley money militia as the "next Steve Jobs." She graduated from high school in Houston, Texas, and was interested in programming and bioengineering.

She started selling C++ compilers to Chinese businesses before she was 19 years old. By 21, she was nearly fluent in Mandarin and was attending school at Stanford, studying chemical engineering. After the end of her first year, Holmes worked in a laboratory at the Genome Institute of Singapore and tested for severe acute respiratory syndrome coronavirus (SARS-CoV-1) by collecting blood samples with syringes (Carreyrou, 2018). She filed her first patent application for a wearable drug-delivery patch in 2003. In March 2004, she dropped out of Stanford's School of Engineering and used her tuition as seed funding for a consumer healthcare technology company. She did all of that before turning 23!

In 2003, Holmes founded Real-Time Cures in Palo Alto, California, to "democratize healthcare for the world." Holmes described her fear of needles as a motivation for future innovations and sought to perform blood tests using only small amounts of blood. Her visionary idea was to eliminate the need to draw vials of blood from anyone and to be able to run "hundreds of tests with only a drop of blood." By looking through her telescope, Holmes could see, at least in her mind, that the future of healthcare was via technology: her technology.

In her microscope, Holmes was focused only on making the innovations work and getting enough money to beat the physics of biochemistry. Even though her professors at Stanford told her directly that what she was working toward was "impossible," Holmes moved closer to her desk and focused even harder on whatever was needed to make her technology work as advertised. Holmes focused on raising money and increased her funding from $3 million to nearly $100 million in one year. Her resolute focus on achieving what she deemed to be true innovations in healthcare drove Holmes to assemble the "most illustrious board" in the history of technology, at least according to the tech bros. In her viewfinder, she could only see the small problem before her; she was blind to the storm of insanity brewing around and within her company.

Holmes' telescopic vision and microscopic focus on making her technology "work" made her forget about the many mirrors she was ignoring. Holmes didn't look at herself in the mirror first and ask, "Why am I doing this? Am I doing the right thing? Is it illegal to do what I am being told to do by my partners? Are my methods taking dollars in funding away from other technologies that might work?" If she had looked in the mirror or adjusted her mirrors for a broader view, her answer would have been, "This isn't the way to do this." Or at the very least, she would have seen the calamities and failures swirling above like hawks waiting to swoop down and strike.

But she ignored the mirrors around her; she never adjusted the aperture of her scopes. She was too focused on falling in love with the attention, grandeur, and media fawning over her. Holmes stayed belly up to her metaphorical desk, eyes squinted, one looking forward at the future and the other surveying her product, knowing her solution was not living up to the hype she was creating. Holmes knew her product was unable to meet her vision. In her telescope, she could see the dream drifting further and further into the abyss of future failure. Holmes was so focused on the microscopic minutia of what was going wrong that she willfully lied and manipulated people to keep the truth hidden. Her dream was impossible, just as she had been told by experts who knew far more than she did, no matter how hard she focused on the problem. The physics of what she was trying to do was beyond the scope of possibility. But when you only view the world through those dual lenses of far-off vision and microscopic product focus, you never see the whole picture. In Holmes' case, that lack of aperture adjustment and hard looks in her mirror cost her over a decade in prison and more than a billion dollars in financial restitution.

I worked with a company where the founder was great at looking through the telescope and the microscope, but he never took the time to look in the mirror. His lack of willingness to adjust the aperture and take that hard look in the mirror ultimately cost his employees a big financial payoff and prolonged the stagnation of this company. For nondisclosure, let's call this company Megacloud. The founder of Megacloud was the original creator of the technology that powered the secure cloud system. This founder was a technologist who started his career working inside the United States Department of Defense. He was the person who coded up the first instances of this capability.

Through his telescope, the founder could see that there was a future in which cloud systems needed to be secure by default. His vision was that his solution would be that default fast cloud configuration engine. And he was not wrong. He was among the first innovators to build automated secure cloud architecture successfully. By looking through his telescope, he realized there was a need in the market, and he saw the route to success where his technology and innovation could benefit the customer.

In his microscope, the founder was focused on enabling anyone using his secure cloud to validate their configuration against security compliance requirements and do so fully automatedly. Although this sounds simplistic, it isn't. Many different compliance initiatives are necessary for a variety of industry verticals. Trying to match them all up in a fully automated fashion is like balancing on a beach ball in the middle of the ocean while configuring a Rubik's Cube. It's hard. Within this founder's microscope, his gaze was focused on making the technology work at all costs. He would move heaven and earth and raise substantial amounts of money to bring this technology to market.

The problem was that this founder, like most other founders I have worked with, had one eye on the telescope and the other on the microscope; because of that, he was missing the more considerable opportunity in the secure cloud market. While his microscopic focus was on enabling compliance via his technology offering, the market was moving toward a state more concerned about automation and the secure configuration of the cloud at scale. And compliance with that cloud instance was, for the most part, optional. The founder's microscopic vision also needed to note that there was a real opportunity to sell his company to acquirers who wanted to take advantage of that more significant secure cloud opportunity. At the same time, this founder's telescope was fixed on his future state where all these moving parts would work in a system that would tap into a potentially more immense multibillion-dollar opportunity. All that focus within the microscope and that long-distance view from the telescope, split between the reality of the market and the founder's future desires for his company, meant the founder missed the current market passing by.

A nearly half-billion-dollar acquisition opportunity fell off the table while the founder stayed glued to his different eye-pieces. An acquisition at that time in that market would have been life-changing at a company with only 110 employees. But the founder was anchored to his microscope and telescope; nothing could divert his gaze. Even when a Hail Mary acquisition opportunity came along, larger than all the previous ones, the founder could not be bothered to entertain the discussion. I wasn't in the room when the offer for the purchase was made, but the company CTO (a great friend of mine) gave me the details.

The buyers offered nearly $600 million for the company in total. But the founder smirked and said, "We are a billion-dollar company. That's the number I'll sell for." According to the CTO, the buyers giggled audibly at that bold, boastful statement and left with an abrupt shrug. Fast-forward 18 months, and the market sailed right by the founder and his ideas. The company valuation dropped through the floor as what was once a genuinely innovative idea became a commodity requirement for cloud systems. The company still exists today. It still has roughly the same number of customers and the same number of employees.

The founder's telescopic vision was forward-looking, but opportunity is a fickle mistress. The founder's microscope view on making his cloud the only one that could automate cloud compliance at the scale he thought the market needed made him ignore the larger, more immediate opportunity.

Had the founder stopped and looked in the mirror more regularly, he would have seen that his vision and view were only self-aggrandizing. Had he adjusted his mirrors and at least looked at things from a different angle, he would have seen that while he was innovative, the market dictates what buyers are interested in. Finally, if the founder had looked at his reflection in the mirror, he would likely have noted that his ego was getting in the way of helping his employees achieve life-changing financial windfalls.

Telescopes and microscopes are powerful tools. They can help us see beyond what is directly in front of us and illuminate the most minor details of unknown elements. But they are only as good as the mirrors that make them function. People often forget you can adjust those mirrors and gain a different perspective.

One can also take a step back, look in a mirror directly, and ask hard questions. To be an effective leader, it is critical that we continually adjust our view and are always open to looking at ourselves in the mirror and asking why we are motivated to do something. Instead of only asking, "Can we?" we should also ask, "Why am I doing this?" Even if you step away from the potential dollars and cents of innovations in the technology market, the real point of the space is to use technology to solve problems. In the Holmes case, technology that might have helped humanity died on the vine and will never see future development. Cloud technology that would have helped small and midsized businesses in the case of the founder I knew stagnated and has proven to be niche in the market. Their approaches to problems could have been game changers, but because they only saw things through those limited views, they let the real opportunities pass them by.

15

Proof Is in the Pudding

Hope begins in the dark, the stubborn hope that if you just show up and try to do the right thing, the dawn will come. You wait and watch and work: you don't give up.

—Anne Lamott

So far in this book, I've talked mostly about the wrong things to do. In this space, I've provided as much insight as I can from my experiences and from analyzing the history of technology leaders to help you understand where things go wrong. As I stated at the beginning of the book, there is immense value in that. But I also think it's never good to dwell only on the negative side of any equation. Therefore, I want to give you examples of companies doing things the right way but differently from the methods of typical technology founders.

Ricardo Villadiego is different, and he has a different background from any technology CEO or founder I have ever met. I guarantee that if you put him in a room with 500 other people and ask someone to pick out a successful cybersecurity and technology entrepreneur, he would not be one of the first chosen. Honestly, that's something for Ricardo to take pride in, if you ask me. Ricardo goes by RV, so that's what I'll call him.

RV is an interesting guy. When he greets you, he always has a genuine big smile. But something behind his eyes lets you know he's always thinking and evaluating everyone and everything he comes across. RV is direct with his questions. When he wants to know something, he asks. RV doesn't, at least in my experience, play games, tolerate fools, or treat people in any way other than how they deserve to be treated. RV exemplifies the CEO character traits that I wish more founders had. But as I said, he isn't the typical Silicon Valley CEO or technology founder. And his background provides some insight into why he doesn't fit the mold.

RV was born in Cartagena, Colombia, a small city in the north of the country. He was raised there until he was roughly 15. RV then moved to Bogota to study engineering. Shortly after that, he finished a degree as an electrical engineer. Following graduation, he went to work for Unisys in Colombia. Even as a student, RV had begun to show his work ethic and tenacity by working for Unisys while still attending school full time. Unisys saw his focus and rewarded his efforts with a leadership position in the company, where he went on to lead a team that helped build software for ATMs and other devices.

During his time at Unisys, RV realized that the protocols he was working with created security issues for Unisys customers, especially those in the banking and finance industry. That realization prompted him to seek new work within Unisys as part of its budding security practice in Philadelphia. He started working with colleagues to build a strategy for security capabilities within the Unisys product suite that ended up in customers' hands globally. Seeing the opportunity that security work offered, RV noticed that Internet Security Systems (ISS) had become one of the big names in security. He left Unisys to work for ISS to capitalize on that growth opportunity for his career. ISS was acquired by IBM in 2006. After the acquisition, RV had seen enough of the corporate world and decided to branch out independently and begin his entrepreneurial life.

Roughly three years later, RV started his own company, Easy Solutions, in Bogota, Colombia—far from the technology hub of Silicon Valley and thousands of miles from the easy money that typical technology founders have access to. RV founded his company with only a few friends, his wife, and a mound of credit card debt. His vision for Easy Solutions was to be the global leader in electronic fraud prevention. It was a grand vision for anyone, especially someone from a Latin American country, where developing technology solutions isn't a typical business opportunity.

RV began by hiring talented developers in the Bogota area to fulfill that vision. His team set out to implement a system to help banks and financial institutions contextualize the totality of fraudulent activity and, therefore, have a higher likelihood of stopping fraudulent transactions. Easy Solutions began selling and operating in its backyard in Latin America.

The company ignored the U.S. market, even though that was the larger pot of gold. The customer adoption and media coverage RV's company earned by serving an underserved market garnered interest in Easy Solutions from international analyst firms like Gartner and Forrester, as well as the media. The follow-on coverage in reporting by those analyst firms and media led to deals in the United States and the rest of the world.

RV was patient and thoughtful about how Easy Solutions went to market. It took his developers and co-founders nearly three years to gain the traction they were after. They didn't start with massive VC funding. RV and his people knew they were on the right track and were building something visionary in its inception that met an immediate market need. They funded the company with revenue and financing from their savings accounts and credit cards. That allowed RV and his team to remain in control of their destiny and not devalue their company as they made gains.

At the time, in the security world, especially in the highly regulated banking arena, no one was buying from Colombian security companies. So, RV and his team adapted to the market demands and offered monthly contracts for early buyers. Once their solution proved itself, his team converted those customers into long-term, multiyear contracts. By 2012, Easy Solutions was off to the races and had over 100 customers and millions in revenue. RV and his team took their wins and sold the company to BC Partners and Medina Capital.

You might take this as a story about overcoming adversity and winning. RV and his team did that, and they should be damned proud of it. But you should also note that RV and his compatriots followed many of the points I've mentioned in this book—and they did so before I ever wrote the dang thing.

RV is a calm, quiet, but direct leader. He asks for what he needs help with, and he gets things done. RV has regular meetings with his team, he doesn't treat them like mushrooms, and he has never in my experience dumpster chickened on anyone or anything in the company. Neither has his leadership team. He surrounded himself with doers who operated independently but for the company's greater good, he trusted them to get things done, and they did—exceptionally well.

He and his leadership team didn't tolerate disrespect and understood that they would get what they expected from their employees. They set high but reasonable goals and continually communicated with the whole company based on the company's needs and growth challenges. His team didn't chase unicorn status and was genuinely not worried about a billion-dollar valuation, although I am sure they wouldn't have been mad if they made it into the club. It simply wasn't a driving force for them. RV and his leaders ate what they killed along the way and didn't take money simply because they could. His team stayed in control of the ship and was strategic, frugal, and innovative, and they won because of it. Finally, they were patient and didn't try to bring a turd into the market and polish it.

They let their work and customers do the talking for them and allowed the analyst firms and media to help them gain market share—not the other way around. RV and his team are a shining example of what, in my opinion, good, honest, authentic leadership in a technology company looks like. If you want to succeed, be like them.

And although it might seem as though RV and his Easy Solutions team's success was a one-off, that's not the case. RV and his team have started another company, Lumu. And they're repeating the same successes with an almost formulaic methodology.

Lumu is working to solve the contextual analysis and insight problems of small and mid-sized businesses in cybersecurity, and they're doing great at it. He has brought along many of the same players who helped make Easy Solutions so successful, and they're rinsing and repeating their success. His head of marketing, Maria, is a dynamo at branding and speaking truth to value. She leads her team with an open conversation style that focuses on delivering value to the customer, not simply beating their competition or owning market share. She leads with kindness and insight far beyond her years in a male-dominated space, and Lumu is already gaining ground in a crowded marketplace thanks to her and her teams' efforts. Maria and her team are so skilled at what they do that Lumu is now ranked as a leader in various analyst reports, and they have done so on a shoestring budget.

RV's lead developer and crew are likely some of the most gifted and innovative solutions builders on the planet, and most of them are from Colombia. Their ability to innovate exceeds others in the cybersecurity space and is always aligned with the operational needs of their customers; they aren't just building something because they can. Anything they take to market is fully operational and focuses on integration and meeting customer needs via integration, not simply adding more technology to the customer stack.

RV has also brought on some heavy-hitting sales leaders and industry leaders from former government spaces who are opening doors and acting as the brand champions the company needs. Lumu is growing well and is on pace to maintain a nearly 84 percent year-over-year growth rate. It won't be long before more good things happen for the company, and rightfully so.

I have no vested interest in Lumu other than that I like to see good people do good things. My points here are untainted. But I know a good leader and team when I see them. RV and Lumu have all of that, and they're following the nontraditional but intelligent approach to success that we need more of. I have been a fly on the wall in some of Lumu's meetings and was invited to its sales kick-off to speak, and that was where I noted the last point I want to make. I have been in hundreds of meeting rooms and sat through more than my share of sales kick-offs and training sessions, but what I saw with the Lumu team stood out.

Everyone at Lumu is always genuinely engaged. The leaders of each group were clearly in command of their respective areas of responsibility, yet no one in the room ever seemed out of their depth, and there was never any positional authority flexing going on. All the conversations I heard or was involved in were measured and respectful. The company troops seemed genuinely aware of the "why" of things, and everyone knew their part in the more significant play. Finally, when it wasn't work time, and everyone was "playing," there was genuine friendship. It was one of the best examples I have seen of what a company should look like when it is led by the right people.

Another company that doesn't fit the traditional technology startup model is ThreatLocker. Danny and Sami Jenkins, husband and wife, run the company.

Right away, that is an unusual leadership model. ThreatLocker is the only company I have encountered managed and led by a husband and wife (and Danny's brother Michael is the company CTO). Building a company valued at near-unicorn status is a family affair at ThreatLocker. The company has been doing everything wrong according to legacy concepts of technology founding and leadership.

Danny and Sami started ThreatLocker nearly a decade ago by receiving a $50,000 accelerator investment from Mach37 in Sterling, Virginia. Even then, I remember Danny and Sami being told in no unclear terms that "a husband and wife should not run a company together." But they were not swayed in their vision and focus for the company.

When Danny brought his brother Michael on, again he was told that "leading with family in the executive suite is a bad idea." But Danny and his family soldiered on despite the guidance of experts at the accelerator firm.

Danny had already founded and sold two other cybersecurity technology firms, but because his approach was outside the norms of established practice, many other folks in the space didn't think a third win was in the bag. ThreatLocker's oddity continues from there, however. Danny and Sami aren't from Silicon Valley; they aren't even American. He is from the United Kingdom, and Sami is from Ireland. Not the usual places one finds technology entrepreneurs. ThreatLocker wasn't founded in a garage in San Francisco; Danny and Sami started and ran the company from Orlando, not far from Disney World. Nothing about ThreatLocker matches up with a "successful" technology company. It's an aberration, but the company excels because of Danny and Sami's dedication and leadership.

Danny is a passionate worker. He continually out-hustles any three people, and expects his employees to be at least as dedicated to the company as he is, but he keeps his approach to their level of effort in check. You won't see Danny criticize anyone for not keeping up with him. He knows himself well enough to understand that he is the draft horse and pulls the largest share of the load, but the others pulling the wagon had better at least tug along with him. Sami is a calm and measured doer who helps ensure that the logistics and functional operations of the company happen smoothly. Michael drives the development and customer support side of ThreatLocker. Each of the leaders at ThreatLocker makes known who they are, what they do, what they bring to the table, and what their expectations are, and then they let their employees do the needed jobs. There is no micromanagement. People do their jobs, aspire to win for the company, are rewarded, and repeat the process. If employees can't keep up or are bad fits, they're shown the door.

Danny, Sami, and Michael don't tolerate laziness or a lack of execution; everyone knows it. The trio set the standard for effort and know how to hold people respectfully accountable. There are no words minced with Danny, Sami, or Michael.

What you see is what you get, and there are no unclear expectations. Employees are motivated and rewarded based on merit and output. ThreatLocker gave a Porsche and a brand-new Tesla to their highest performers last year on top of bonuses and stock awards. Danny and Sami know what motivates people and work to ensure that their employees are rewarded justly. When a company trip needs to happen, Danny allows employees of all ranks to ride on his company jet if space is available. Although it seems like a strange benefit to offer, from a leadership perspective, it's brilliant because it makes employees feel valued—and everyone wants to fly private. You never see a person leave the ThreatLocker jet in a bad mood.

ThreatLocker didn't receive funding for years, even though the company grew by 200 percent quarter over quarter. Danny and Sami had VCs beating down their doors to take an investment round. However, until ThreatLocker, its product, and its market traction were fully aligned, Danny and Sami stayed focused, executed, and grew sans VC money.

They, too, ate what they killed and were wise to avoid chasing big enterprise deals. ThreatLocker focused on selling to the managed security service provider (MSSP) market and leveraged that scale to grow the company's client base. Sure, ThreatLocker took an enterprise deal when it came the company's way, but that was never the focus of the team's efforts.

There are no dumpster chickens at ThreatLocker. Danny, Sami, and Michael have all been in the trenches and done the work. When a need arises for top cover or expert-level assistance, the leadership team dives in and helps or guides the execution. No mushroom farming is done, either. Danny and the team are clear about what they expect, and they let the company rank and file know what is happening and why things are taking place. Communication is always clear and concise. That clarity lets everyone know which way the winds are blowing and helps the crew right the ship when the need arises.

Finally, Danny and Sami don't follow the typical technology market mantra of letting their employees work from anywhere just because it's possible. They do have some employees who work remotely for specific purposes, but ThreatLocker moves its employees to Orlando whenever possible. This requirement helps them maintain better oversight on productivity, encourages interactions, and grows company comradery. Danny and Sami knew this and made it a point to buy and furnish their company building in Orlando, specifically with those values in mind.

ThreatLocker's leaders have done everything differently. But because of Danny and Sami's measured and insightful approach to running a technology company, ThreatLocker is succeeding. Even in the current economic downturn, its last valuation was near unicorn status, and the company continues to hire new people and grow.

The leadership teams at ThreatLocker and Lumu are living proof that success happens if a company and its leaders stick to their guns and execute. Their ability to effectively lead and manage their businesses and employees ultimately wins the day.

There is no magic formula for doing things right, especially in leadership. But there is immense value in knowing what pitfalls to avoid and understanding where you can and will go wrong. I am sure there are a hundred other aspects of leadership that I could have written about in this book, but I know that what I've shared can directly benefit anyone who reads it. Good companies and good people can and do fail for various reasons. My genuine hope is that by reading this book, you can see the failures I've described as cautionary tales, that you never act as a dumpster chicken or a mushroom farmer, and that as a result, you can craft your success.

References

"15 Employee Productivity Statistics You Want to Know." 2023. Retrieved from www.apollotechnical.com/employee-productivity-statistics

Aivazpour, Z. and Valecha, R. 2021. "The Impact of Data Breach Severity on Post-Breach Online Shopping Intention." Retrieved from www.researchgate.net/publication/334726367_The_Impact_of_Data_Breach_Severity_on_Post-Breach_Online_Shopping_Intention

Basysta, J. and Kyslova, K. 2020. "How to Correctly Estimate Your App Development Timeline." Retrieved from https://proxify.io/articles/how-long-does-it-take-to-develop-an-app#don-t-rely-on-rough-app-development-time-estimates

Bradberry, T. 2009. "The Cost of Seagull Management." Retrieved from www.emerald.com/insight/content/doi/10.1108/00197850910950925/full/html

Bradberry, T. 2016. "Are You A Seagull Manager?" Retrieved from www.inc.com/travis-bradberry/are-you-a-seagull-manager.html

Brown, D. 2018. "Why You Shouldn't Aim to Reach Unicorn Status." Retrieved from www.inc.com/david-brown/why-you-shouldnt-aim-to-reach-unicorn-status.html

Burda, M., Genadek, K. R., and Hamermesh, D. S. 2016. "Not Working at Work: Loafing, Unemployment and Labor Productivity." Retrieved from www.nber.org/papers/w21923

Burenko, S. 2022. "How Long Does It Take to Make an App?" Retrieved from www.uptech.team/blog/how-long-does-it-take-to-make-an-app

Caldwell, F. 2021. "Prediction 2021: Vendors Fail to Deliver on IRM." Retrieved from https://thansyn.com/prediction-2021-vendors-fail-to-deliver-on-irm

Carreyrou, J. 2018. *Bad Blood: Secrets and Lies in a Silicon Valley Startup.* Alfred A. Knopf.

Claburn, T. 2020. "Remember When Netscout Got so Upset at 'Challenger' Label in Gartner Magic Quadrant, It Sued? Well, Top Court Just Ended All Those Shenanigans." Retrieved from www.theregister.com/2020/01/16/netscout_gartner_lawsuit

Clarke, J. 2012. "Titanic Disaster: How History Has Judged Bolton's Sea Captains." Retrieved from www.bbc.com/news/uk-england-manchester-17678822

Daugherty, G. 2020. "What Was the Titanic's Captain Doing While the Ship Sank?" Retrieved from www.history.com/news/titanic-captain-edward-smith-final-hours-death

Deloitte. 2016. "Why Do Projects Fail?" Retrieved from www2.deloitte.com/us/en/insights/deloitte-review/issue-19/why-projects-fail.html

D'Este, C. 1996. *Patton: A Genius for War*. Harper Perennial.

Farr, C. 2015. "Why Homejoy Failed." Retrieved from www.wired.com/2015/10/why-homejoy-failed

Flashpoint Intel Team. 2021. 2021 Year End Report - Data Breach Quick Review. Retrieved from https://flashpoint.io/blog/2021-data-breach-report

Galford, R. M. and Drapeau, A. S. 2003. "The Enemies of Trust." Retrieved from https://hbr.org/2003/02/the-enemies-of-trust

Genter, J. 2020. "How Airlines Make Billions From Monetizing Frequent Flyer Programs." Retrieved from www.forbes.com/sites/advisor/2020/07/15/how-airlines-make-billions-from-monetizing-frequent-flyer-programs/?sh=e99ec7d14e91

Gleason, S. and Mann, T. 2015. "Invention Startup Quirky Files for Bankruptcy." Retrieved from www.wsj.com/articles/invention-startup-quirky-files-for-bankruptcy-1442938458

Goffee, R. 2017. "The Best Leaders Are Constant Learners." Retrieved from https://hbr.org/2017/05/the-best-leaders-are-constant-learners

Gotsis, G. 2020. "5 Reasons Why Flat Organizational Structures Fail." *Journal of Management Development*, 1286–1301.

Group, B. C. 2018. "Decoding Global Talent: 200,000 Survey Responses on What Fuels Employee Engagement." Retrieved from www.bcg.com/en-us/publications/2018/how-to-keep-your-top-talent/decoding-global-talent-2018.aspx

Halligan, B. and Shah, D. 2014. *Inbound Marketing: Attract, Engage, and Delight Customers Online*. John Wiley & Sons.

Hershfield, H. E., Mogilner, C., & Barnea, U. 2016. People who choose time over money are happier. *Social Psychological and Personality Science*, 7(7), 697–706. journals.sagepub.com/doi/abs/10.1177/1948550616649239

Herschfield, H. 2023. *Your Future Self: How to Make Tomorrow Better Today*, Kindle edition. Little Brown Spark.

Heskett, J. 2014. "Can the Brilliant Jerk Be Managed Effectively?" Retrieved from `https://hbswk.hbs.edu/item/can-the-brilliant-jerk-be-managed-effectively`

Huczynski, A. A. 2013. *Lack of Clear Structure and Hierarchy: The Pros and Cons of a Flat Organizational Structure*. Pearson Education Limited.

Huczynski, A. A. and Buchanan, D. A. 2013. *Organizational Behaviour*. Pearson Education Limited.

Identity Theft Resource Center. 2022. "16th Annual Data Breach Report." Retrieved from `www.idtheftcenter.org/post/identity-theft-resource-center-2021-annual-data-breach-report-sets-new-record-for-number-of-compromises`

Jennings, R. 2009. "Gartner Sued by ZL re. Magic Quadrant; Huge Damages Claim." Retrieved from `www.computerworld.com/article/2467990/gartner-sued-by-zl-re--magic-quadrant--huge-damages-claim.html`

Johnson, R. E. 2014. "Getting to the Core of the Matter: Workplace Relational Civility and Its Influence on Employee Well-Being." Retrieved from `https://doi.org/10.1037/a0034263`

Kotler, P. T. and Keller, K. L. 2007. *Marketing Management*. Pearson Learning Solutions.

Kerner, S. M. 2002. "34 Cybersecurity Statistics to Lose Sleep Over in 2022." Retrieved from `www.techtarget.com/whatis/34-Cybersecurity-Statistics-to-Lose-Sleep-Over-in-2020`

Kerr, S. 2019. "The One Thing You Need to Know About Managing Gen Z Employees." *Harvard Business Review*.

Kitterman, T. 2023. "5 Ways Workplace Culture Drives Business Profitability." Retrieved from `www.greatplacetowork.com/resources/blog/5-ways-workplace-culture-drives-business-profitability`

Kruse, K. 2018. "The One Thing Successful Leaders Never Do." Retrieved from `www.forbes.com/sites/kevinkruse/2019/04/02/10-surprising-things-successful-leaders-do-differently`

Lagorio-Chafkin, C. n.d. "What Happened to Quirky?" Retrieved from `www.inc.com/video/how-a-niche-product-tapped-into-a-global-market.html`

Lee, C. T. 2017. *NetScout Systems, Inc. v. Gartner, Inc. Memorandum of Decision re Defendant's Motion for Summary Judgment* (Docket Entry No. 305). Retrieved from `https://casetext.com/case/netscout-systems-inc-v-gartner-inc-4`

Lohrman, D. 2021. "Data Breach Numbers, Costs and Impacts All Rise in 2021." Retrieved from www.govtech.com/blogs/lohrmann-on-cybersecurity/data-breach-numbers-costs-and-impacts-all-rise-in-2021

Lomas, N. 2019. "Most EU Cookie 'Consent' Notices Are Meaningless or Manipulative, Study Finds." Retrieved from https://techcrunch.com/2019/08/10/most-eu-cookie-consent-notices-are-meaningless-or-manipulative-study-finds

Madden, S. 2015. "Why Homejoy Failed . . . And the Future of the On-Demand Economy." Retrieved from https://techcrunch.com/2015/07/31/why-homejoy-failed-and-the-future-of-the-on-demand-economy

Mayhew, H., Saleh, T., and Williams, S. 2016. "Making Data Analytics Work for You—Instead of the Other Way Around." Retrieved from www.mckinsey.com/capabilities/mckinsey-digital/our-insights/making-data-analytics-work-for-you-instead-of-the-other-way-around

Moldes, C. 2019. "Compliant but Not Secure: Why PCI-Certified Companies Are Being Breached." Retrieved from https://csiac.org/articles/compliant-but-not-secure-why-pci-certified-companies-are-being-breached

Morris, K. 2023. "Here's How Many Hours Workers Are Actually Productive (and What They're Doing Instead)." Retrieved from www.zippia.com/advice/average-productive-hours-per-day

National Archives. n.d. "The Story of Captain Edward John Smith, Captain Titanic." Retrieved from www.nationalarchives.gov.uk/titanic/stories/edward-john-smith.htm

O'Reilly, C. A. 2013. "Organizational Ambidexterity: Past, Present, and Future." *Academy of Management Perspectives*, 27 (4): 324–338.

Porath, C. L. 2007. "Does rudeness Really Matter? The Effects of Rudeness on Task Performance and Helpfulness." *Journal of Management*. Retrieved from https://doi.org/10.1177/0149206307302554

Privacy Affairs. 2022. "GDPR Fines Tracker and Statistics." Retrieved from www.privacyaffairs.com/gdpr-fines

Project Management Institute. 2018. Pulse of the Profession: "Success in Disruptive Times—Expanding the Value Delivery Landscape to Address the High Cost of Low Performance." Retrieved from www.pmi.org/-/media/pmi/documents/public/pdf/learning/thought-leadership/pulse/pulse-of-the-profession-2018.pdf

Pros and Cons of a Flat Organizational Structure. n.d. Retrieved from www.indeed.com/career-advice/career-development/pros-and-cons-of-a-flat-organizational-structure

Shanthi, S. 2022. "Is Achieving Unicorn Status No Longer a Mark of Success?" Retrieved from www.entrepreneur.com/en-in/news-and-trends/is-achieving-unicorn-status-no-longer-a-mark-of-success/440354

Shapiro, E. 2020. "Netflix's Reed Hastings on Rejecting Brilliant Jerks, the Power of Big Vacations, and Spending $15 Billion on Content." Retrieved from https://news.yahoo.com/netflix-reed-hastings-rejecting-brilliant-105003901.html

Society for Human Resource Management. 2016. "Employee Job Satisfaction and Engagement: Revitalizing a Changing Workforce." Retrieved from www.shrm.org/hr-today/trends-and-forecasting/research-and-surveys/Documents/2016-Employee-Job-Satisfaction-and-Engagement-Report.pdf

Statista. 2023. "Average Number of New iOS App Releases per Month from March 2019 to June 2023." Retrieved from www.statista.com/statistics/1020964/apple-app-store-app-releases-worldwide

Sutton, R. I. 2007. *The No Asshole Rule: Building a Civilized Workplace and Surviving One That Isn't.* Business Plus.

Thompson, A. 2022. "Biden's Top Science Adviser Bullied and Demeaned Subordinates, According to White House Investigation." Retrieved from www.politico.com/news/2022/02/07/eric-lander-white-house-investigation-00006077

Verizon. 2022. "2022 Verizon Data Breach Investigations Report." Retrieved from www.verizon.com/business/en-gb/resources/2022-data-breach-investigations-report-dbir.pdf

Voss, J. 2018. "Jawbone: From Innovative to Insolvent." Retrieved from https://cmr.berkeley.edu/2018/04/jawbone-startup-failure

Wilkinson, M., & Hamilton, R. 2011. *The Story of the Unsinkable Titanic.* London: Transatlantic Press.

Willink, J. and Babin, L. 2017. *Extreme Ownership: How U.S. Navy SEALs Lead and Win.* St. Martin's Press.

Zeitlin, M. 2019. "Why WeWork Went Wrong." *The Guardian.* www.theguardian.com/business/2019/dec/20/why-wework-went-wrong

Acknowledgments

The list of people I want to acknowledge as great leaders and examples of how one should lead an organization is far too long. I have been blessed to know, meet, and work with various people across the industry who are true bastions of what we need more of in the executive suite. Although I can't possibly list them all, I would like to thank a few directly:

- Greg Touhill
- John Kindervag
- Heather Dahl
- Stephanie Balaouras
- Joseph Blankenship
- Jeff Schilling
- Jon Brandt
- The Ft Meade CPO mess
- The team at Forrester Research Security Group
- Godard Abel
- Sara Rossio
- Chris Voce

There is a long list of others that would fill up another book. Thank you for guiding me and helping me know what *good* and *great* looks like for people in leadership roles.

I would also like to thank the amazing team at Wiley for helping get this book over the line and for taking a chance on a crazy title.

Finally, I want to thank my family for their patience as I wrote this and for dealing with the days of having a less-than-mentally functional dad in the house, because my brain dump here was substantial. Thank you for your support and love.

About the Author

Known in the cybersecurity industry as "Dr. Zero Trust," Dr. Chase Cunningham is the creator of the Zero Trust eXtended framework and a cybersecurity expert with extensive experience in all aspects of enterprise security, including decades of operational experience working in various capacities supporting NSA, US Navy, FBI Cyber, and other government mission groups. He served as chief strategy officer at Ericom Software, was VP of Security Market Research at G2, and was a Forrester Analyst. Additionally, Dr. Cunningham held several positions at the U.S. Navy as a Chief Cryptologic Technician, as well as other civilian corporate roles as the director of threat intelligence for Armor and director of cyber analytics for Decisive Analytics. He is the author of the *Cynja* series, *Riptide*, *gAbrIel*, and *Cyber Warfare: Truth, Tactics, and Strategies*.

Index

use of term in technology
space, 151
U.S. Navy SEALs, "Slow is
Smooth, and Smooth is
Fast.," 77

V
venture capital (VC)
deciding whether or not to
take cash injec-
tion of, 96–97
as easy to get but there is a
sucker born every
minute, 104
funding in, 94–95
as helping technology
companies move fast but

there is always a price to
be paid, 102–103
Villadiego, Ricardo
(RV), 175–180

W
Wallace, Rachel, 89, 90
The Walt Disney
Company, 86
WeWork, 159–160
Wistia, on flat organizational
structure, 63

Z
Zak, Paul, 26
Zappos, on flat organizational
structure, 61